Training Guide

PageMaker 4.0 for Windows

Bart Milner

PITMAN PUBLISHING

Pitman Publishing
128 Long Acre, London WC2E 9AN

A division of Longman Group UK Limited

First published in 1993

British Library Cataloguing in Publication Data
A CIP catalogue record for this book can be obtained from the British Library.

ISBN 0 273 60181 4

Printed in England by Clays Ltd, St Ives plc

Contents

Introduction

Welcome to PageMaker, probably the most user-friendly of all the professional desktop publishing (dtp) systems. It is, in the view of many users, a program that meets many of the standards of professional layout and typesetting, but unlike some other computer programs, it is quite easy to learn and use.

Dtp requires a software package such as PageMaker 4 (PM4) to lay out texts and graphics for publication. By creating layouts on the screen, dtp can give the experienced user fast, cheap and flexible control over their work to produce a printed document of professional quality.

Although PageMaker is user-friendly, it is capable of producing professional results: both *New Scientist* and *MacUser*, large, glossy, well-produced magazines, are amongst the many professional publications using the program. PageMaker's popularity in publishing is partly because it has, for a long time, been available on both Macintosh and IBM-compatible computers, and it is actually fairly simple to translate a Macintosh PageMaker file into the IBM format. Competing packages have struggled, and sometimes failed, to be available for both systems.

PageMaker provides you with the tools to combine text and graphics. Text can be prepared on a wordprocessor beforehand and imported into the dtp program, but this is not usually necessary since the big advantage of PM4 over earlier versions of the program is that it has a good basic text editor (the *Story editor*) built in.

Graphics can also be imported, from drawing/paint packages, borrowed from a clip art library or copied into memory using a scanner. Although PM4 is not designed to be used as a drawing program it has a very reasonable range of drawing tools and effects which can produce some very professional-looking designs. Professional users often use desktop scanners to provide an image on the screen or on their proofs, but including scans of photographs (halftones) can be difficult because of the huge amount of computer memory that even small halftones require.

PM4. like most dtp programs, represents the physical layout area with an image of a piece of paper on screen, accompanied by a box of design tools. After selecting a design tool, the mouse is used to move about on the page image and carry out a particular task, such as inputting text, changing type style and size, or importing a picture.

PageMaker is unlike other 'frame-based' desktop publishing packages which require that all text and graphics must be placed in a *frame*, an area of the working page marked off for text or picture placement. Professional designers are accustomed to using frames because this is how almost all conventional layout is done, with each block of text typeset on to a separate piece of paper (a *galley*) which is physically glued on to a pre-designed grid. However, those coming to dtp without a background in layout find it easier, in general, to move and size the different components of a page layout on the page itself and this is how, at least in the initial stages, PageMaker works.

If you have any experience with other dtp programs you will probably expect to find text or picture boxes. PageMaker has both, but rather than waiting on a pre-designed page, they are attached to each piece of text or picture as it is imported on to the page. They are also extremely flexible and can be stretched in all sorts of different ways to fit the layout that you want.

One of the major advantages of dtp is that text and page design can be updated and corrected immediately, without extra cost apart from the labour involved. Changing a design or text which has been typeset conventionally is both slow and extremely expensive. PageMaker exploits this flexibility by making it very simple to resize pictures and to change the shape, size and format of text.

Pictures in a well-designed layout make all the difference between a professional-looking publication which attracts attention and a bald block of text which people will only read if they have to (like most official forms).

If you do not have a scanner to create pictures, you can get quite good results by simply photocopying your artwork and using a photocopier which will scale it to the right size. Then cut and paste it into the right place on the page after you have printed out your dtp text.

The combined text layout and picture(s) can then be copied again for distribution, since photocopies are much cheaper than laserprints, or given to a printer to convert into plates for output on a small web offset machine (the cheapest way of printing 200 or more copies).

PageMaker does incorporate advanced editing facilities to provide cross-referencing and indexing for long publications. These are not dealt with in this *Guide* because you should become familiar with all the basic functions and commands of PM4 before you attempt to layout a long document. In general, short sections or chapters are much easier to handle than long ones.

Although PageMaker will accept hundreds of pages in a single document, you are strongly advised not to create a publication in this way, since short files are much easier to save than long ones and mistakes can be remedied much more easily. You can tie these sections together, and number consecutive pages for example, using the **Book** command: consult your manual for detailed instructions on how to go about this.

PM4 for Windows

In the past, IBM-compatible DOS (the disc operating system) has been a big problem for dtp, because dtp generates and uses many, very large files. DOS is inherently inflexible and unfriendly, partly because it is very powerful, and in order to make life easier for ordinary users, the Windows environment was developed.

Windows is an interface between machine and user designed to simplify use. It was strongly influenced by the extremely friendly environment developed for Apple Macintoshes. Windows sits on top of DOS and as a result it has some strange quirks, but generally speaking Version 3.1 works quite well.

This is not a manual about Windows, but it does describe some basic file management techniques that are essential when dealing with dtp documents. One important thing to know about Windows is that each task has its own area of the screen (hence window) which can open when you need to do a particular job. The bigger your machine, the more windows and applications you can have running at the same time. If you start to get a lot of error messages, or the machine appears to be behaving erratically, in most cases it is not a virus, you simply have too many windows open and should start closing them down.

Learning dtp

One of the problems that many people encounter with dtp is a sense of confusion caused by the huge number of choices the program gives them. As soon as you open a menu, you find many options and sub-menus available. Do not be put off, you certainly do not have to learn all of PM4's available options before you can produce good quality work. Very few users know all the different options that PM4 can provide.

Generally, PM4 has an extremely sensible and useful series of *defaults:* automatic settings which come with the program. These can all be changed very easily but you will find it simpler, in the early stages, to leave them alone unless instructed otherwise by this *Guide*. When you are comfortable with what a given option can or cannot do, you can experiment with changing the defaults.

The reason that there are so many options is that typesetting and layout is a complex and highly skilled craft. If you have never done a layout before you will probably start to notice just how many and varied are the different styles used in printing. PM4 (and other professional dtp packages) can now mimic virtually all the technical capabilities of typesetting and conventional layout which apprentices, until quite recently, spent up to seven years learning. This is a lot for the beginner to take on, and even experienced users are continually discovering new aspects of dtp.

When laying out a page, you should remember that reading is hard work for most people and a large part of your job is to make it as easy as possible for the reader. Broadsheet papers (like the *Independent* or *Daily Telegraph*) have designs and layouts which expect the reader to work much harder than tabloid newspapers, such as the *Daily Mirror* or *Sun*, which have four or five times the circulation of the broadsheets.

Layout is always a balance between using pictures and graphics to get the attention of the reader in the first place, getting as much information on one page as possible (to save printing and paper costs), and using large type and lots of white space so that the page is easy to read.

Although PM4 is easy to learn and use it will not necessarily teach you how to produce a well-designed, professional-looking layout. PM4 is a superb tool which can help you develop these skills, but each page of layout is unique, and learning to operate a dtp program is not the same as learning how to design an attractive spread of type and pictures. This takes practice.

Remember to save constantly and to back-up your files. The Learning Resources Computer Centre at London College of Printing and Distributive Trades has a notice up which reads: **'Guarantee. These machines are guaranteed to fail when you least expect it. Save your work as often as you can'.**

PM4 is a large program but it rarely crashes on the Macintosh. The IBM-compatible disk operating system (DOS) is not so reliable and rather more prone to crashing. If this occurs, PageMaker will try and rescue your file and store it (consult your manual about how to try and retrieve it) but it is much better to save frequently and then you will lose very little work when the inevitable happens. To avoid repetition, this *Guide* does not always tell you to save every time you complete a portion of your work, but if you get into the habit of doing so you will save yourself a great deal of work in the long run.

Because of the complexity of dtp, everybody at some point gets into a mess they cannot get out of. The best thing to do then is to use the **File, Revert** command or the **Revert** to mini-save described on page 37, which will reopen your file at the last point it was saved. This makes it particularly useful to save as soon as you have reached a point where your work is in good shape. It is good practice to use the **Save as...** command at the end of a session. The reasons for this are technical, but essentially it cleans up all the deleted text and changes which are usually hidden but still present in the file. It is essential to do this if you are converting a file from an earlier version of PageMaker or transferring across from Macintosh to IBM format (or vice versa). You can use the original file name by clicking in the file window to select it.

Installation

This training manual assumes that Windows 3 (or a later version) and PageMaker 4 (PM4) have already been installed on your machine. Consult your manuals on how to use the Aldus Setup if you need to install PM4. It is worth checking, particularly on a machine used by others, which filters have been installed. These filters enable PM4 to read files created in another application. Use Aldus Setup to install or remove these filters, they take up a lot of RAM (*memory*) and you should remove them if they are not required.

Acknowledgements

This manual was prepared with a great deal of very generous help from **Mr Brazil and Carmen Garcia** of **The Printing Centre, London WC1, Ian Monk** and **Adam Whitehouse.** Special thanks also to **Peta Howlett** of **Lemon Graphics** and **Alex Watson** of **The Printing Centre,** who have never failed to find an answer to my technical questions and to the HND Business and Finance (Journalism) students at London College of Printing and Distributive Trades who taught me a great deal, not least how much fun teaching PageMaker can be. Pictures were prepared using evaluation copies of the Snagit and Tiffany screen-dump programs, supplied by shareware specialists Omicron System Ltd (0702 710391).

Thanks also to Aldus for supplying a demonstration copy of PM4 and for creating such a good program. This book was entirely laid out in PageMaker 4 from which 600 dpi camera ready copy was supplied using a Hewlett Packard LaserJet 4.

Getting started

Throughout this *Guide*, the following terms will be used to describe operations with the mouse:

POINT: MOVE the mouse to position the pointer on the screen to SELECT menus, menu options, tools etc.

CLICK: PRESS the left-hand button on the mouse quickly and release it (unless the right-hand mouse button is specified).

DOUBLE CLICK: PRESS the left-hand button on the mouse twice in quick succession.

TREBLE CLICK: PRESS the left-hand button on the mouse three times in quick succession.

DRAG: CLICK and HOLD DOWN the mouse button whilst moving the mouse to a new position.

SELECT: To select, POINT to an item, such as frame, menu option, tool etc. and CLICK.

HIGHLIGHT: Selection is in reverse video (black areas turn white and vice versa) to indicate that a current menu option, desktop tool, or section of text has been selected. File names are highlighted with a single CLICK and can be activated or opened with a DOUBLE CLICK. Text is highlighted with a CLICK and DRAG mouse action. DOUBLE CLICK on a word to HIGHLIGHT it. TREBLE CLICK to HIGHLIGHT a paragraph.

OK: Most options have an OK box on their menu. POINT to this and CLICK to action the options you have selected or PRESS [Enter] on the keyboard.

PLACE: Use the **Place** command to import a file into a publication.

TOGGLE: CLICK on an option to TOGGLE on or off. Menu options usually have a tickmark next to them to indicate when they are toggled on. Many dialogue box options have a button (circle) next to them, which turns black when toggled on (active), and white if they are toggled off.

SCROLL: CLICK on the scroll arrow or box to open or move down a pulldown menu and SELECT an option.

CANCEL: Some options present you with a menu in which there is a cancel box — POINT to this and CLICK the button on the mouse, if you wish to close an option (dialogue) box without making any changes.

REPEAT: Repeat the previous step or steps indicated in an Activity.

The mouse controls the screen pointer and cursor. MOVE the mouse to position the screen pointer and then CLICK when you are in the right position on the screen. With the pointer tool selected, clicking will select the nearest item to the screen pointer. With the text tool selected it will place the the cursor in position. Use the right-hand mouse button when you need to toggle between **Fit in window** and **Actual size**.

PageMaker allows you to have items stacked on top of each other in layers. If you have trouble selecting an item because it is covered by another item, press the [Ctrl] key and continue to CLICK with the mouse. This will take you through the different layers, selecting each item in turn.

Sub-menus are indicated in this *Guide* by a comma after the main menu entry e.g. **File, New**. POINT to the menu on the **Menu bar**, and then to an item in the sub-menu in the pulldown box which opens up. A comma after a sub-menu indicates an option.

All keyboard strokes in this *Guide* are indicated by a box around the relevant key name, e.g. [Alt], [Enter]. Note that where keys are to be pressed simultaneously they are boxed together with a plus sign, e.g. [Alt + F] ; where they are to be press sequentially, they are presented in sequence, e.g. [Alt] [F].

Windows gives you a keyboard shortcut for virtually all menus, sub-menus and options. This is indicated by a letter underlined in each entry on the screen. PRESS the [Alt] key and the letter for the main menu, followed by the letter for the sub-menu or option.

Opening PM4 Switch on disc drive and screen. When the Windows' Programe Manager appears go to the PageMaker icon and click the left-hand mouse button twice in quick succession.

This is called double clicking. It can be a bit of a knack getting the timing of double clicking right, and old mice which have been heavily used can be a bit temperamental so you may need to practise this a few times.

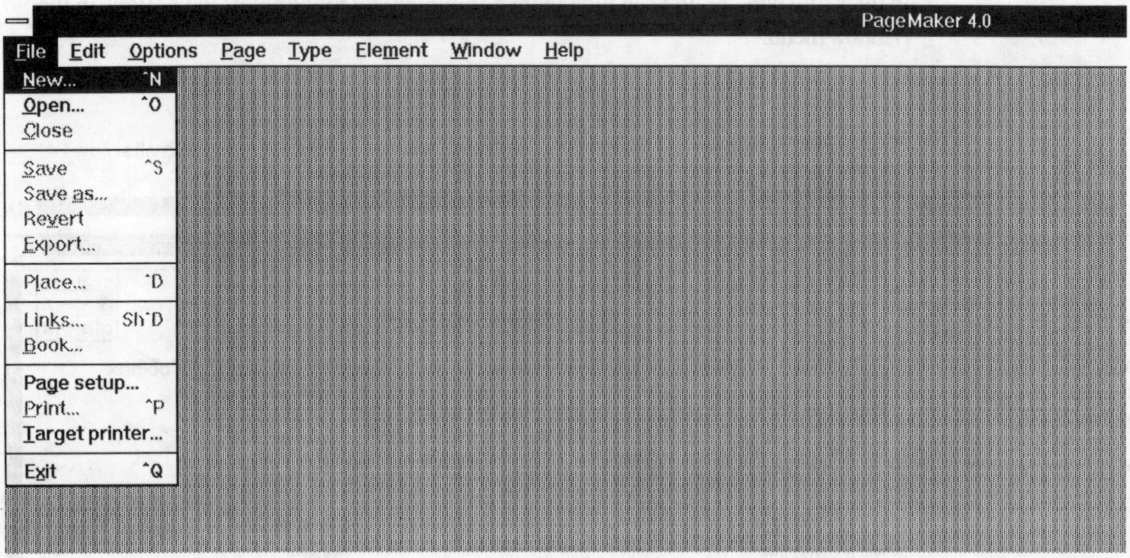

When the program has loaded, your screen will be blank apart from the **Main menu**. POINT the mouse at **File** and CLICK. The **File menu** will appear. CLICK on **New...** (the first entry).

The following dialogue box will appear. Options in each box will depend on PM4's defaults or the last settings chosen. PRESS Enter.

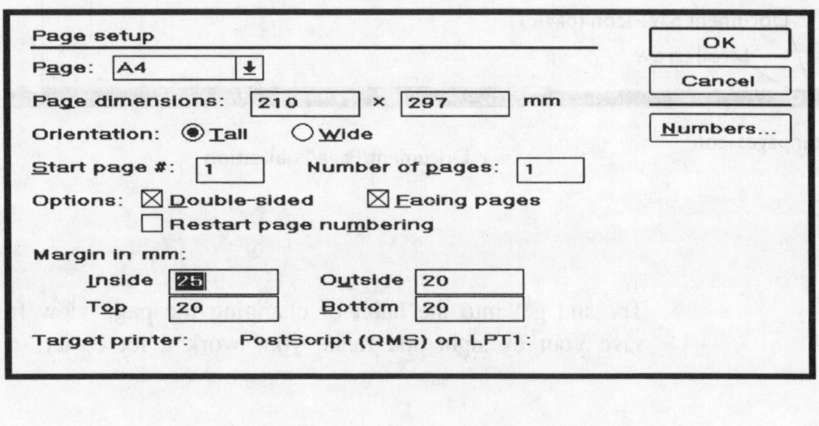

The large white area on the screen is PM4's representation of a blank page, referred to as a 'publication'. On this page you can input text and graphics (pictures). The usual printer page size is A4.

Unless you have a very large screen, you will often find that you need to see more of a document than is currently on view. You can determine how much of the document is displayed by using the right-hand mouse button or the **Page menu** (*see* below) but you can also move the Toolbox (and the Style and Colour palettes) by clicking and dragging on their title bars, or you can hide them completely by toggling off the options in the **Windowmenu**.

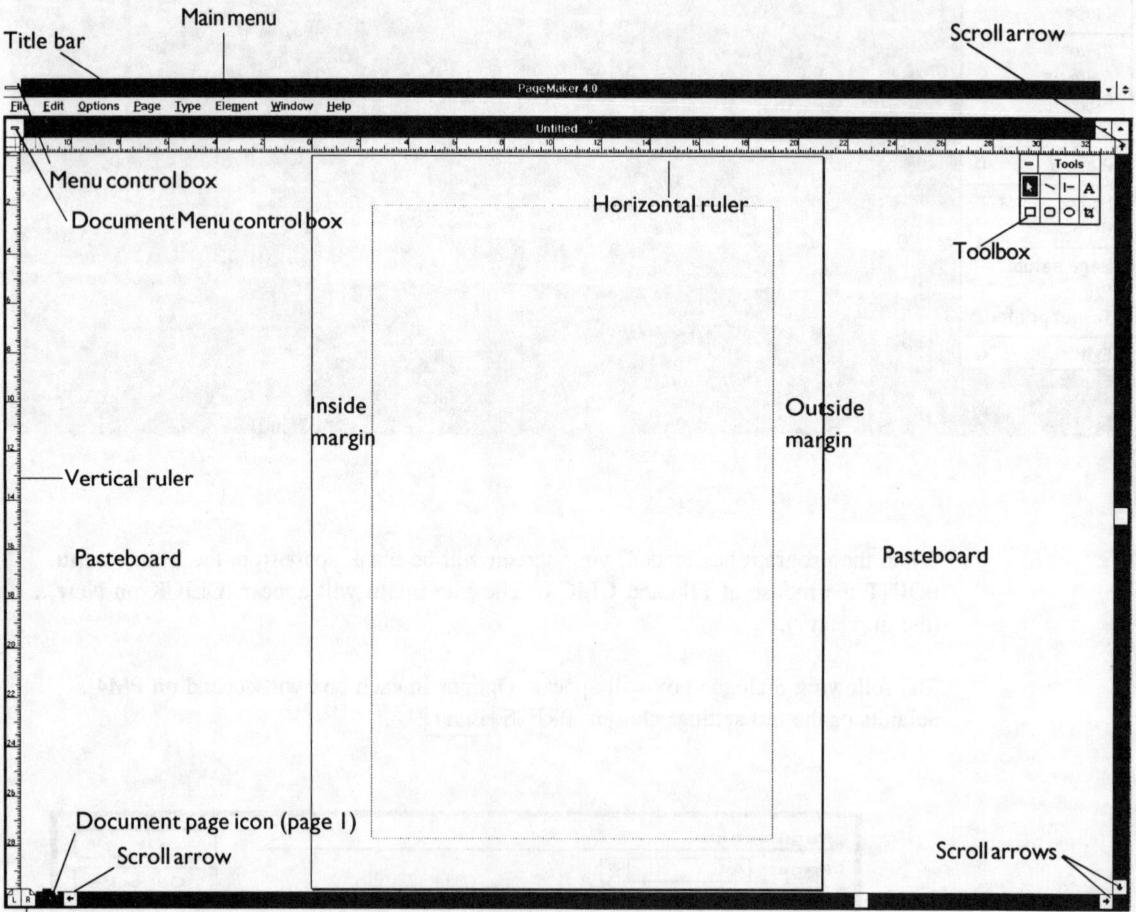

Document/Page/Publication

Try and get into the habit of changing the page view frequently — it will help save your eyesight and make your work a lot easier.

The Help window

PM4 in Windows comes with a **Help** feature which is useful if you have forgotten what a particular command does or where you can find it.

As you begin to understand the program, use the **Help** facility to get more information, or clarify a function. It can save you hours of frustration, but it is surprising how often users forget about its existence.

If you are new to Windows try the exercise below and use the **Help** window to explain the use of **Select all**. Once you can do that, you should not have any difficulty using **Help** whenever you need it. **Help** does not always explain *why* things are done but the Topic list usually explains *how* to operate a function.

1 POINT the mouse at **Help** on the far right of the **Main menu**.

2 CLICK and the **Help** pulldown menu will appear.

3 SELECT **Topics**.

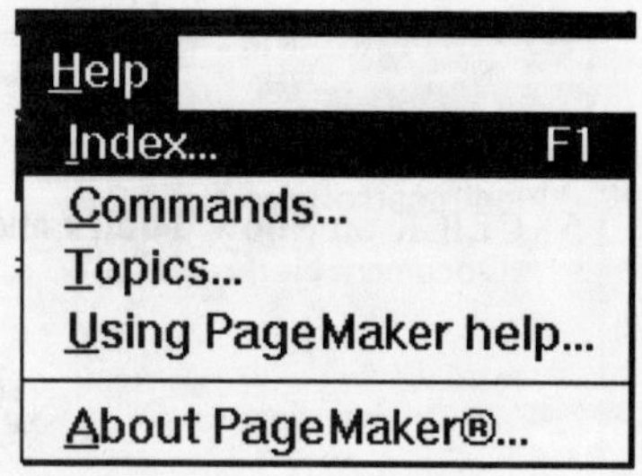

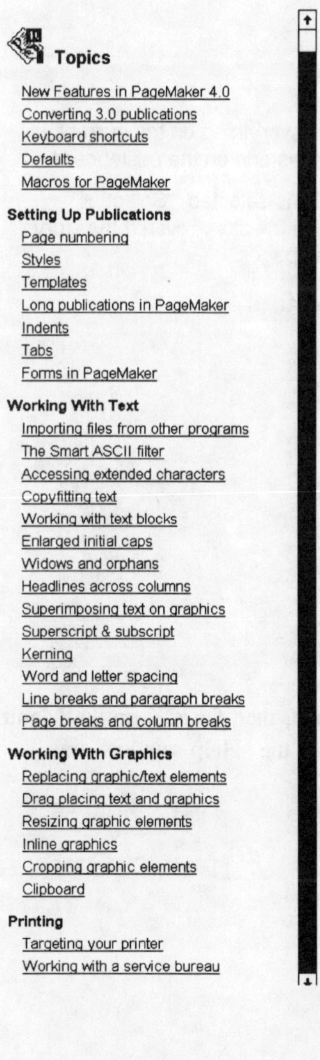

4 CLICK on **Search** and then TYPE **select all**.

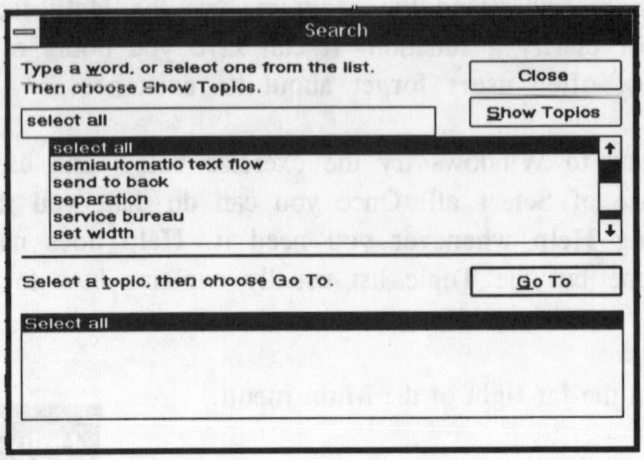

5 CLICK on **Show Topics** and then **Go To**.

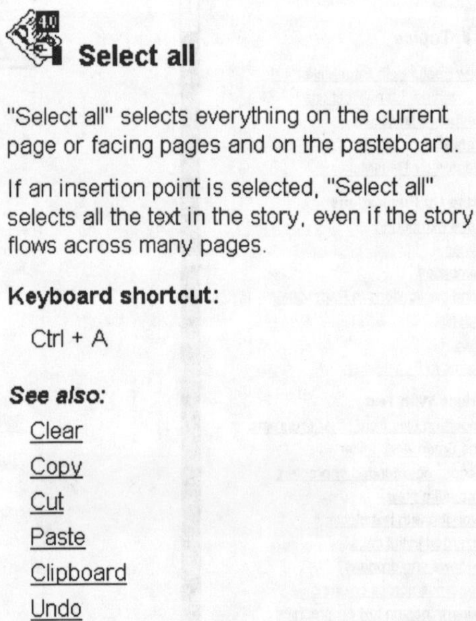

6 POINT at any of the ***See also:*** list to open, then CLICK on the **Menu control** box in the top left-hand corner of the **Help** window and CLICK on **Close**.

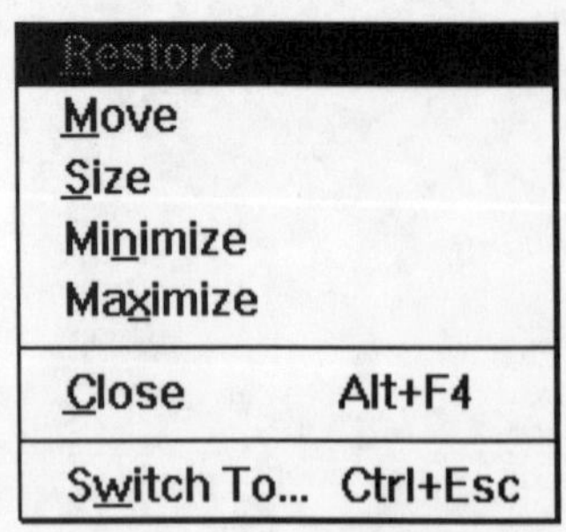

Housekeeping

There are some basic housekeeping dos and don'ts which should help to keep your system trouble-free.

1 Dtp often involves combining a lot of different files from different programs and/or different machines to produce a single publication. It is very important to keep these files in good order with names that you will be able to remember easily. Once you have imported a file into PageMaker using **Place**, you should not move it from one folder (sub-directory) to another and you must not rename it. If you do either of those things, PageMaker will not be able to find the file and although the screen representation may look fine, it will probably fail to print out properly. You can remedy this using the **File, Links...** command (*see* your manual for details) but this can waste a lot of time unnecessarily.

2 It is quite easy to move files on to your hard disc from a floppy and it is important to backup **all** your hard-won documents and associated pictures and text on floppy disc but make sure you observe the two ground rules: do not move files between folders or rename them after placing in a PageMaker document.

3 Make sure that you know how to move your files around in Windows.
This chore is particularly important if you are working with pictures, because they can quickly use up available disc space (if you are using them a lot, a file compression program is a very good investment).

The good news is that Windows has a file management system, **File Manager,** which is much easier to learn than DOS, although it does take a little practice to get used to it. Be careful of the **Control menu** box, if you double click on this accidentally it will close down your application without giving you a chance to save your work.

The **Switch To** Ctrl + Esc command is also very powerful and very useful: it enables you to move to any open application or, open **File Manager** through **Program Manager** (the Windows' opening screen) which is always on the Task List, or open any other application, providing that you have enough RAM to run several applications at once.

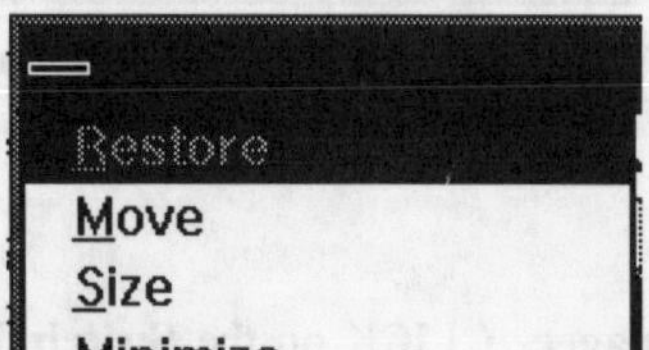

You can also use the **Switch To** command to **Quit** open applications, using the End Task box.

When moving or deleting files you can select consecutive files if you hold down the Ctrl key *after* selecting the topmost file. This can save a lot of time when deleting or copying files, but be careful, accidentally deleting a file, which may have taken hours of painstaking work, happens to even the most experienced users. If in doubt, save and backup, you can delete extra files much more quickly than you can recreate original work.

Do not forget that you can activate many actions in Windows simply by double clicking on the icon or directory entry. All of the **Menu control** options can operate this way.

If you have little or no experience with the **File Manager** try this exercise and use the Menu control box to copy a file after inserting a formatted floppy disc containing the file into drive A or B.

1 POINT at the box in the very top left-hand corner of the document window and CLICK. The **Menu control** pulldown appears.

2 CLICK on **Switch To…**. Your current Task List appears.

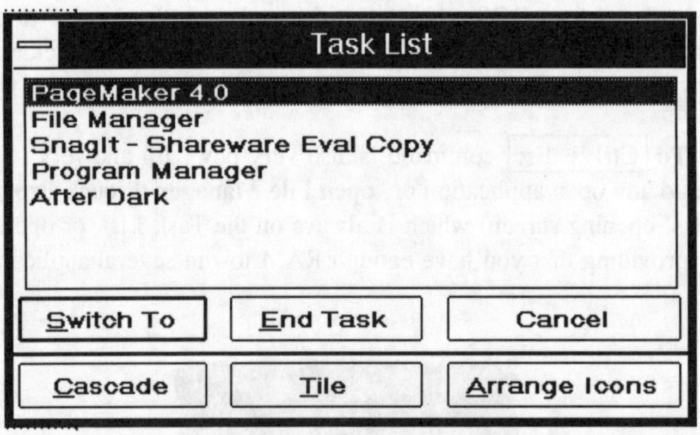

3 CLICK on **Program Manager**. CLICK on the **Switch To** box and the Windows' opening screen appears.

4 DOUBLE CLICK on **File Manager** in the **Main** window and the directory for the C:\ drive will appear. TOGGLE on View, Tree and Directory.

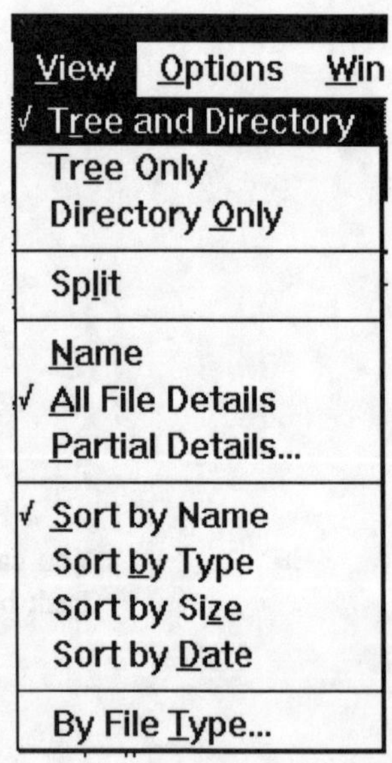

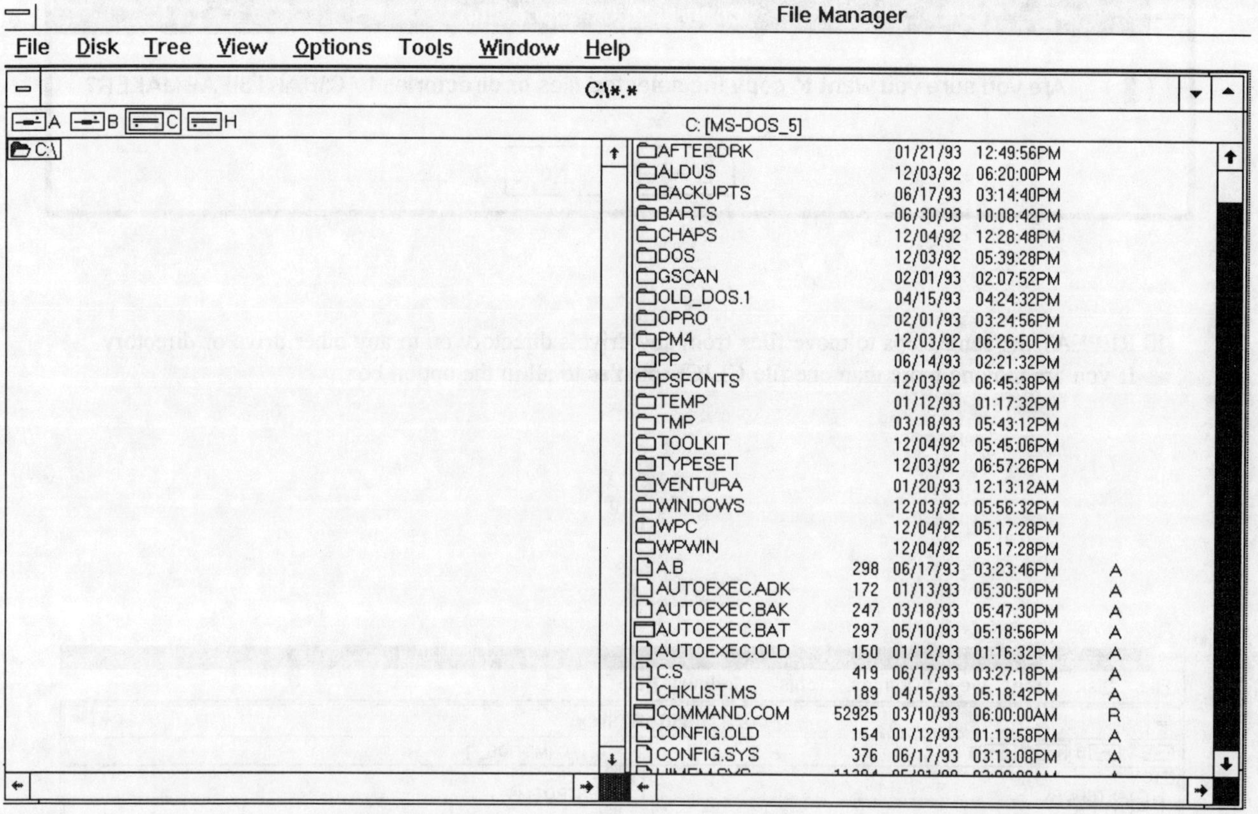

5 DOUBLE CLICK on the A (*or* B) drive icon and a new A:\ (*or* B:\) window will appear. DOUBLE CLICK on the A:\ folder icon and the A:\ (*or* B:\) directory will appear.

6 CLICK AND DRAG on the black **Title bar** marked B:\ (*or* A:\):*.* and DRAG it to the right.

7 SELECT the window containing the directory of your discette: the **Title bar** will be highlighted and the frame on the window will be highlighted. POINT the mouse at the edge of the frame and find the point where the screen pointer changes to a double-headed arrow. CLICK AND DRAG the frame to a convenient size.

8 CLICK on the C drive icon, CLICK on the sub-directory you wish to enter, DRAG and resize window as in step 4 of this activity.

9 CLICK on the file you wish to copy in the directory of the floppy and DRAG across to the selected sub-directory. The screen pointer changes into an icon of a document and a message appears asking you to confirm that you wish to copy the file into the sub-directory of the hard disc. CLICK on **Yes**.

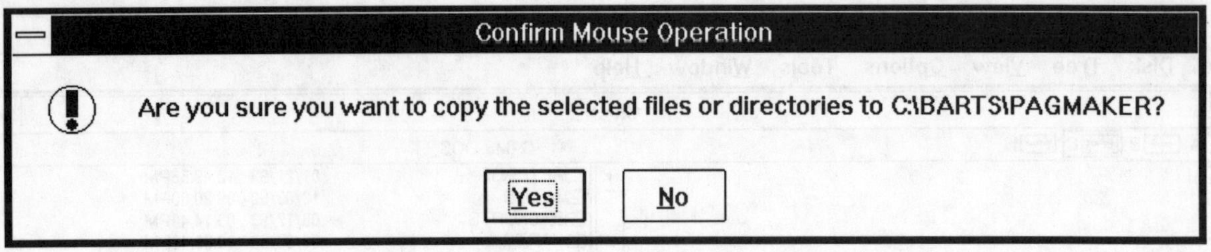

10 REPEAT the same steps to move files from any drive's directory on to any other drive or directory. If you are moving more than one file CLICK on **Yes** to all in the option box.

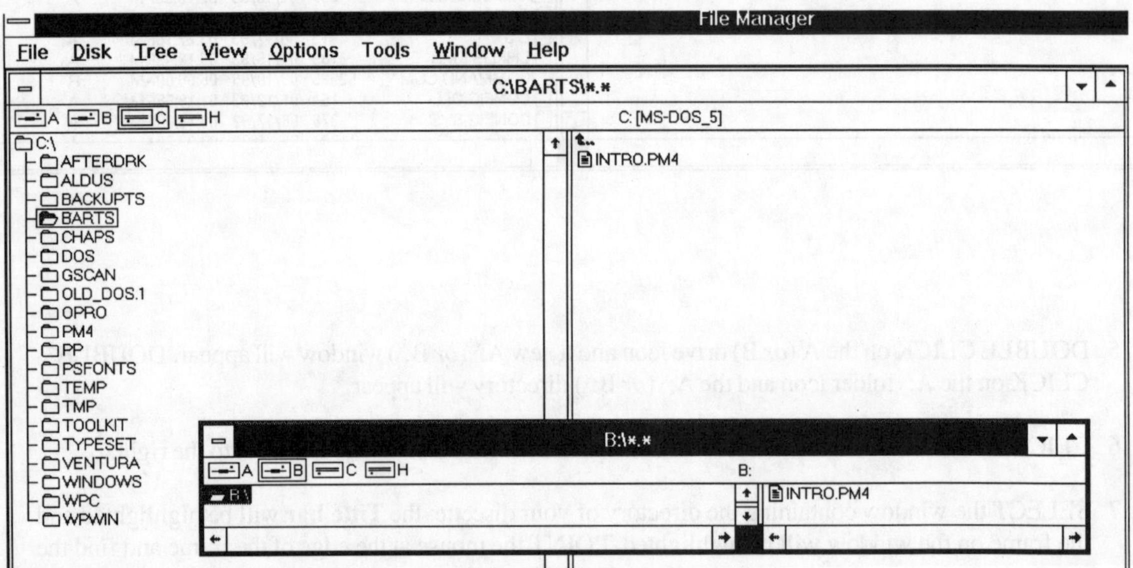

Section A
The basics

Task 1: Reading the screen
Task 2: Saving a document, closing it and quitting PM4
Task 3: Learning to use the Toolbox
Task 4: Simple text formatting
Task 5: Printing a document

Task 1 Reading the screen

➢This task is designed to familiarise you with the different ways of viewing the page on screen

When PageMaker is opened from Windows the screen is usually blank apart from the **Menu bar** and **Toolbox.** To create a new page on screen you must select the **File, New** command from the main menu.

This will give you a complex screen with many choices and options. Do not worry about these, simply move the screen pointer to the OK box and CLICK the left-hand mouse button, and a new page will appear on your screen.

You will then be taking a look at some of the different ways in which you can view that page. This is one of the most important commands for any dtp program, because of the continuous need to view a small portion of the layout to do a particular job and then to view the whole page or spread of two facing pages to see the effect of that job on the appearance of the whole layout.

Using the right-hand mouse button and the screen pointer, you can enlarge (zoom in) to show a portion of your document in its actual size or reduce (zoom out) to fit the whole page into the window.

PageMaker has a very large range of its own keyboard shortcuts and also uses all of the keyboard shortcuts built into Windows. You should start to use them as soon as you can as they will save you a great deal of time later. PageMaker's shortcuts are preferable because they usually require only one keystroke. Windows's shortcuts normally require two keystrokes: the Alt key and another key to open a menu, then another key to select an option or sub-menu.

Activity 1.1 Using the Menu bar to open a new file

1 Use the mouse to POINT the screen pointer on **File** in the top left-hand corner of the PM4 window on the **Menu bar**.

2 CLICK the left-hand mouse button to SELECT **File** and open the sub-menu.

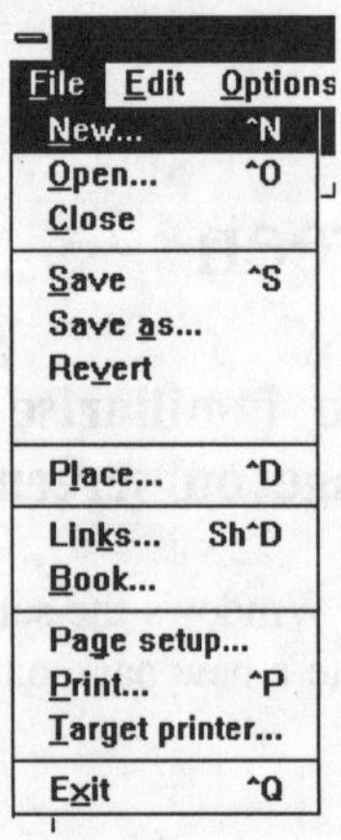

3 DOUBLE CLICK on **New**. The Page setup… dialogue box will appear with default settings in place. If you click **OK** to this, your next screen will be like that on the following page.

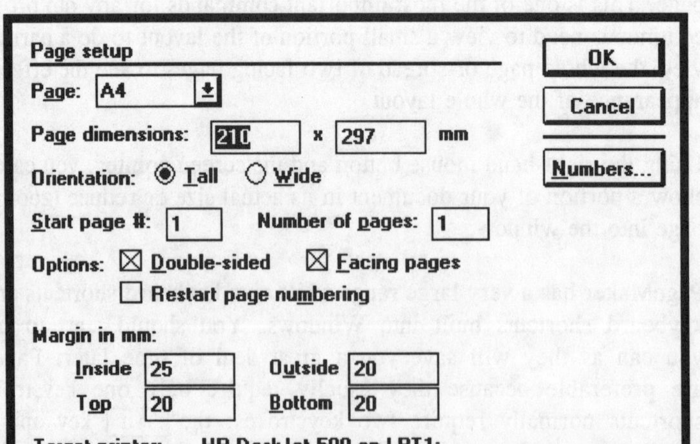

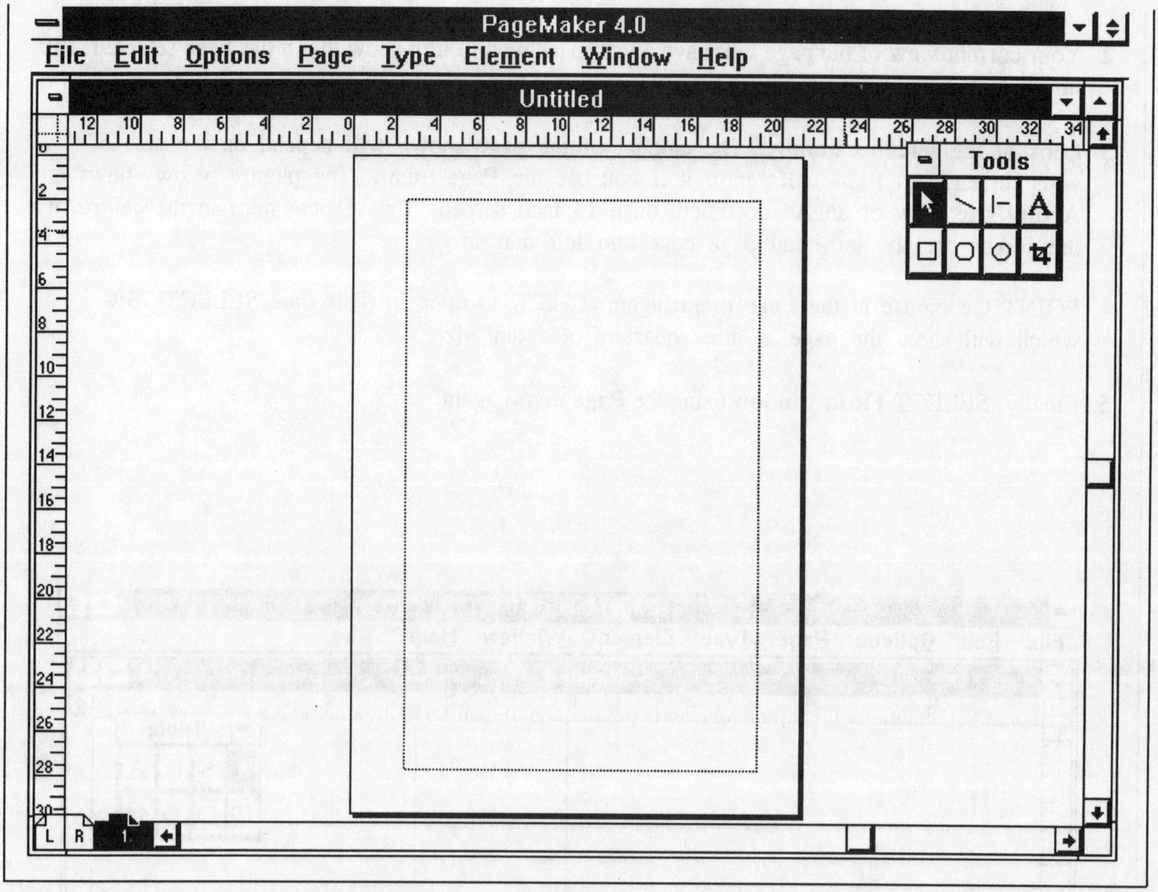

Activity 1.2 Using the Main menu to view the screen

1 POINT the mouse at the **Page** command on the **Main menu**. CLICK to open the **Page menu**.

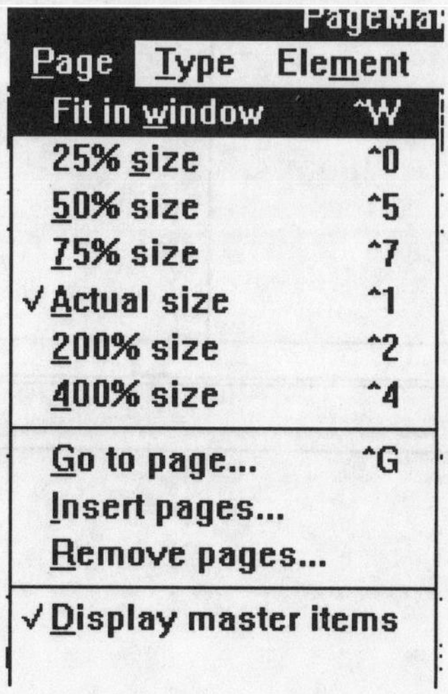

2 Your current view of the page will have a tick mark next to it to show that it has been selected. **Fit in window** is the usual default. POINT the mouse at the **Actual size** option and CLICK.

3 Look at the screen carefully. The amount of the page shown will depend on the size of your screen, and PM4 will centre it if you use the **Page menu**. The picture below shows an **Actual size** view of an A4 document on a 14 inch screen. The vertical lines in the centre of the screen are the left-hand page edge and left margin.

4 POINT the mouse at the **Page menu** again. CLICK to open it. This time SELECT **75%** which will show the page at three quarters of actual size.

5 Finally, SELECT **Fit in window** using the **Page menu** again.

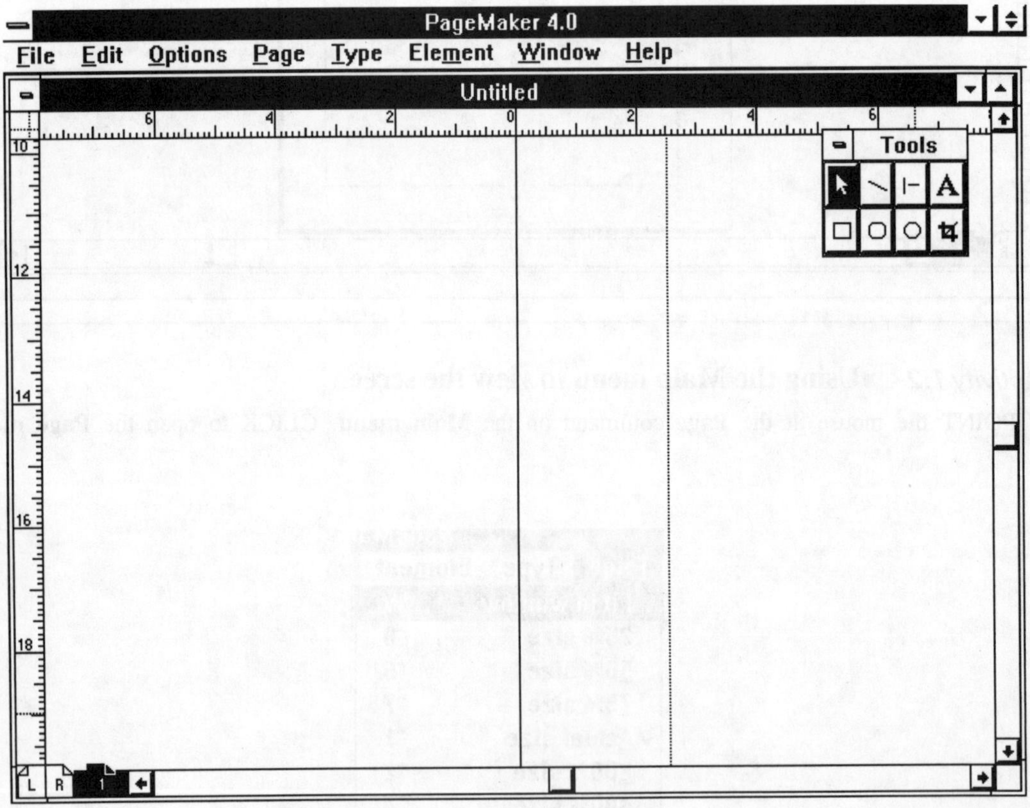

Activity 1.3 Using the mouse to control page view

1 POINT the mouse at the top left-hand corner of the page (not the screen).

2 CLICK with the right-hand mouse button. The window will zoom in to show the page area where you clicked, at Actual size. Use the mouse to position the screen pointer on any part of the page you wish to see enlarged.

3 CLICK the right-hand mouse button again. This will zoom out and return your page view to **Fit in window**. You can TOGGLE between these two views by using the right-hand mouse button.

4 Practise this a few times.

Because you can choose the area of the page you want to zoom into by pointing the mouse at that part of the screen before you CLICK, this is one of the most useful shortcuts in PM4 for Windows.

Activity 1.4 Using keyboard shortcuts

1 PRESS the Ctrl key, hold it down and press **4.** The page view will shift to 400%.

2 PRESS the Ctrl key, hold it down and press **7**. The page view will shift to 75%.

3 POINT the mouse at **Page** and CLICK. The menu lists PM4 keyboard shortcuts in the

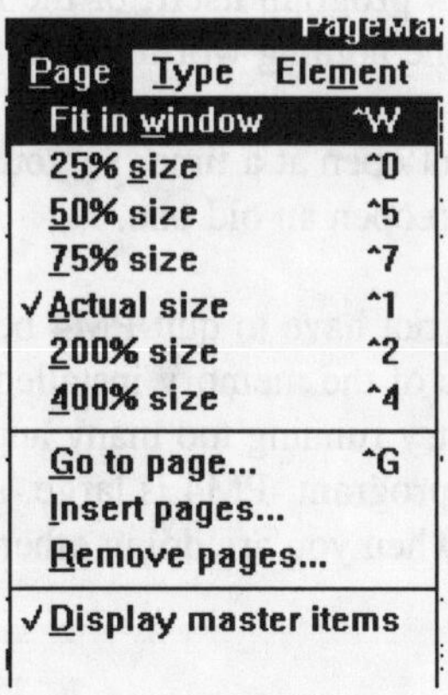

right-hand column. The Ctrl key is represented by a ^ (carat) character.

4 *Note* that the menu items have one letter in each word underlined, including the **Page** command. These are Windows' keyboard shortcuts, which are most useful when PM4 does not have its own shortcut, as in the **Page** option: **Insert pages....**

5 CLICK anywhere on the screen, outside the menu, to cancel.

Task 2 Saving a document, closing it and quitting PM4

➢This task deals with saving a document and quitting PM4

Although you have not yet put anything on your document, you are going to **Save** it to disc.

The reason you need to learn this command immediately, as you may know from other applications, is that the **Save** command is very important — you should use it many times when producing a single document. It is essential to learn the keyboard shortcut (Ctrl + S) and use it often. Layouts are usually complicated pieces of work and it is a very good idea get into the habit of saving them regularly, not when they are finished, but when you have successfully completed any large task.

Save has a twin command, **Save as...**, which enables you to name (or rename) a document and make sure it is placed in the right directory. If you open a new document, you will be taken into **Save as...** when you try to save, to make sure that you do not forget to name it. Thereafter you can use **Save** but when you complete a document use **Save as...** again (*see* Introduction).

After you save a document, you can close it. Do not use **Close** without saving first, unless you wish to throw away your document. PM4 will ask you whether you wish to save changes. If you check the **No** option, then any work you have done since opening the document or since your last **Save** command will be destroyed permanently. You will get a similar alert if you close the PM4 program itself, or the **Program Manager** (Windows). Select **No** only if you have done nothing worth keeping.

PM4 allows you to have only one document open at a time, so your current document will close if you open a new document or reopen an old one.

Windows allows multi-tasking and you do not have to quit PM4 before opening another application. Depending on the size of the memory installed in your machine, you will have problems with RAM if you try running too many applications at once. Although economical for such a powerful program, PM4 is large, so get into the habit of using **Quit** to close down the program when you are doing other things.

Activity 2.1 Saving a document

1 POINT the mouse at **File** and CLICK to open.

2 POINT the mouse at **Save** and CLICK to select.

3 The Save publication as dialogue box will appear:

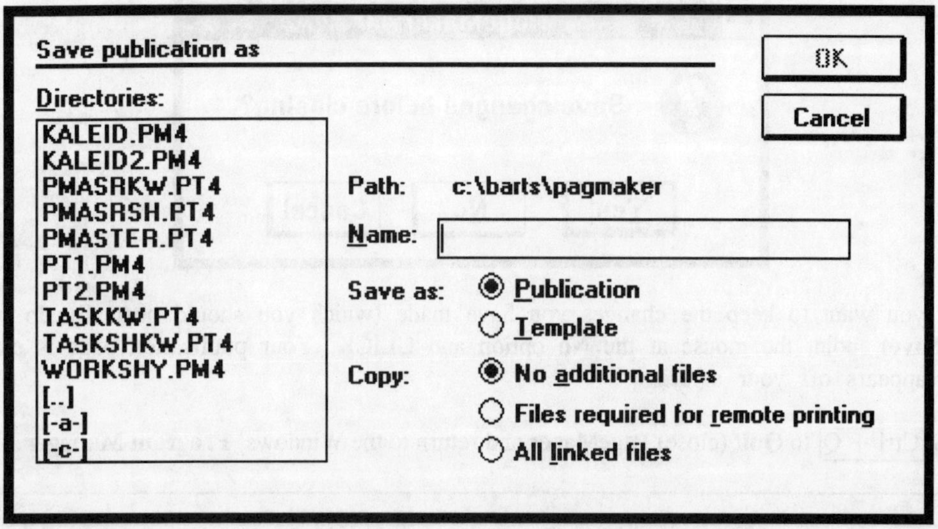

4 TYPE **FIRSTRY** in the Name: box (the text cursor will be flashing to the left-hand side of this box, enabling you to type). POINT mouse at OK and CLICK (the left-hand button).

5 Your document has been saved as **FIRSTRY.PM4.**

PageMaker automatically supplies the **.PM4** extension to your file. If you try to give it another extension, PageMaker will not be able to recognise, and open, your document.

Activity 2.2 Using Windows keyboard shortcuts

1 PRESS the [Alt] key, hold down and PRESS the [F] key. The **File menu** will open.

2 Cancel by clicking outside this menu. PRESS the [Alt] key again, hold down and PRESS the [P] key. The **Page menu** will open. CLICK outside this menu to cancel.

3 You can open any item on the **Menu bar** by using the [Alt] key and an underlined key letter.

4 PRESS [Alt], hold down and PRESS [F] again. Look at the third line of the **File menu** and note that the **Close** option has no PM4 shortcut. PRESS [C] (Do not use [Alt] this time). Once a **Menu bar** item has been opened you can choose almost any option by pressing its key letter, which will be underlined.

5 If you have made *any* changes, however small, the following alert appears on your screen.

6 Unless you want to keep the changes you have made (which you should normally do by using **Save**), point the mouse at the **No** option and CLICK. Your publication page is closed and disappears off your screen.

7 PRESS Ctrl + Q to **Quit** (close) PageMaker and return to the Windows' **Program Manager**.

Activity 2.3 Reopening a document

1 POINT the mouse at the PM4 icon in Windows and DOUBLE CLICK.

2 SELECT **File, Open** on the main menu bar and the following dialogue box will open:

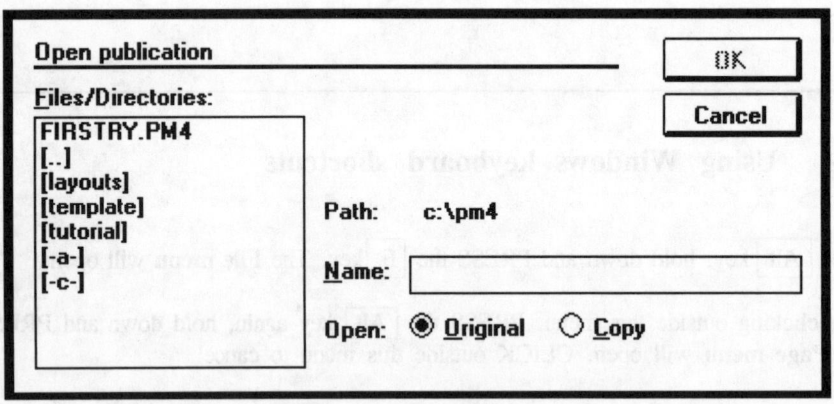

3 POINT the mouse on **FIRSTRY.PM4** and DOUBLE CLICK. The document will open in the PM4 window.

Task 3 Learning to use the Toolbox

➢This task is concerned with using the text and pointer tools

At the heart of PageMaker is the **Toolbox**, which tells the mouse what sort of functions to perform.

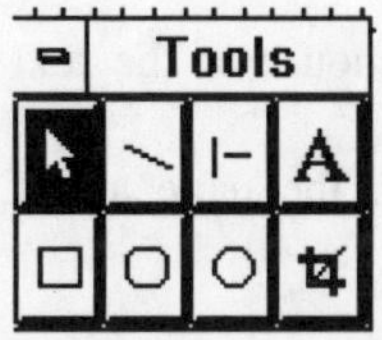

The two main tools in the **Toolbox** are the pointer tool and the text tool. The pointer tool is in the top left-hand corner of the **Toolbox**. It is selected when you POINT the mouse on it and CLICK. After the pointer tool has been selected you can CLICK AND DRAG on an item on the displayed document page to move it to a new position or to change its shape or size.

The text tool is in the top right-hand corner of the **Toolbox**. When it is selected, you can CLICK anywhere on your document and start typing in text.

Most of the problems that people experience when they first learn PM4 are caused by forgetting that you cannot enter text with the pointer tool and you cannot move items with the text tool. Remember to choose the right tool for whatever you want to do.

Unlike other dtp programs, you do not need to draw in a 'text' box before you type in any text in PageMaker. PM4 draws its own invisible text boxes as you type in text. You will see this if you select the pointer tool and then CLICK on some text. The text box will appear on the screen.

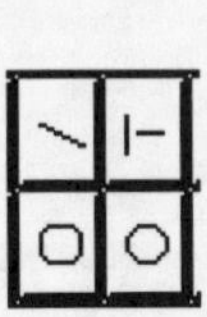

The other tools in the **Toolbox** are graphics tools: you can use them to draw basic shapes, such as lines, rectangles and ellipses. To draw straight lines, squares and circles, you need to hold down the Shft key while you CLICK AND DRAG with the mouse. This will constrain the graphics tool that you have selected so that it only draws symmetrically.

The sixth tool in the bottom right-hand corner of the **Toolbox** will be dealt with later in this book. It is the cropping tool, which acts like a pair of scissors (or a scalpel) to cut pictures to fit a given space on the page.

Activity 3.1 **Using the text tool, entering text and saving a document**

1 In **FIRSTRY.PM4**, POINT the mouse at the text tool and CLICK to select.

2 POINT the mouse (anywhere) on the page and CLICK. The screen pointer will turn into a blinking cursor.

3 CLICK with the right-hand mouse button. The page shown on screen will be enlarged to **Actual size**.

4 TYPE in your name and address, pressing Enter at the end of each line (you don't need to reposition the cursor for each new line).

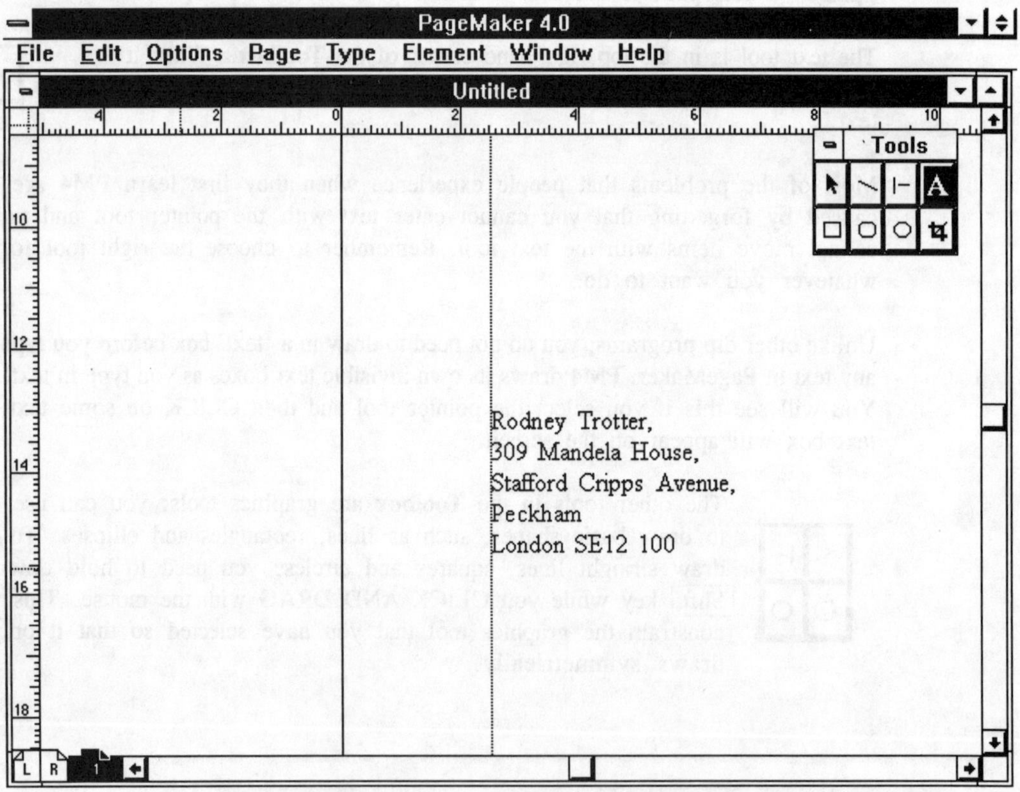

5 CLICK the right-hand mouse button again; the on-screen page will revert to **Fit in window**. Your text will now appear as grey lines (*greeked*) unless you have a large (A3+) screen.

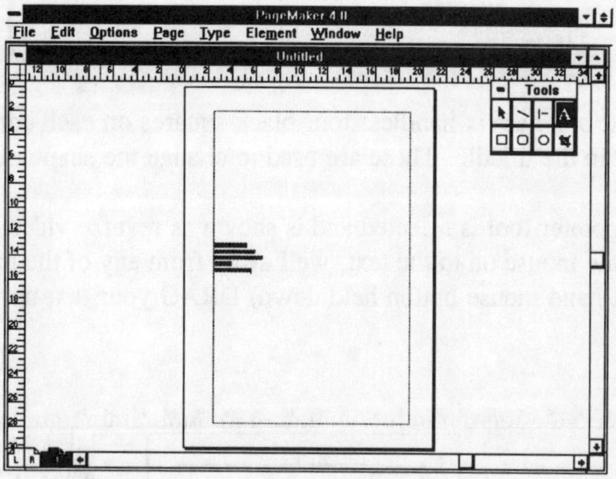

6 PRESS Ctrl + S , the screen will flicker and your document will be saved under its old name (**FIRSTRY.PM4**).

Activity 3.2 Using the text tool to move a text box

1 SELECT the pointer tool. POINT the mouse in the middle of your text and CLICK to select.

2 A text box (only displayed when the pointer tool is selected and is clicked inside the text area) will appear. CLICK on it with the right-hand mouse button to zoom in on the text area. *(You must CLICK on or very close to the text box or you will zoom into the wrong place on the page.)*

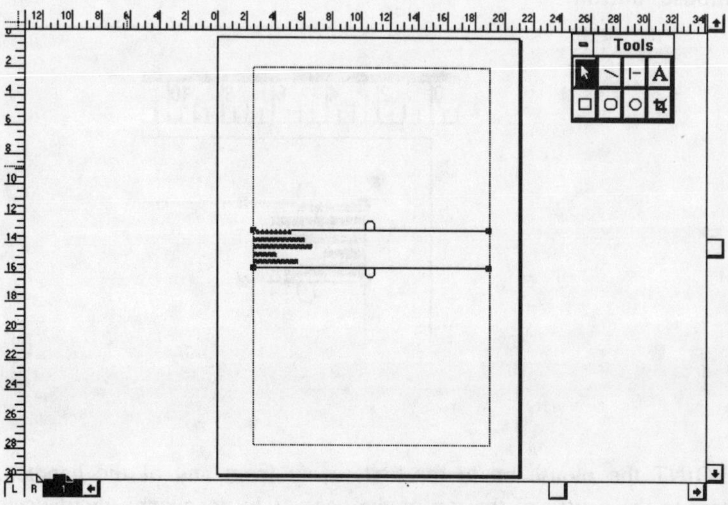

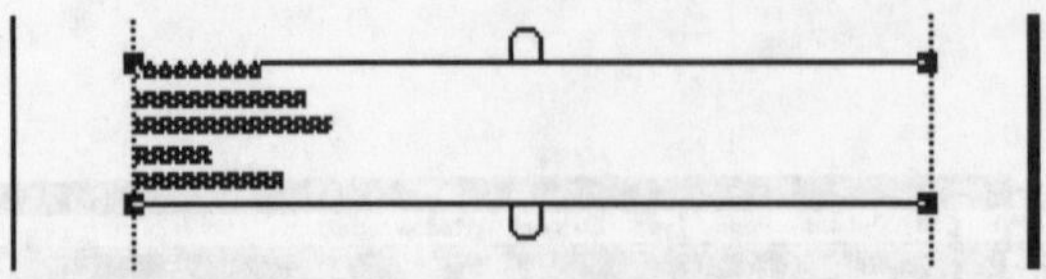

3 Note that the text box has six handles: four black squares on each corner of the 'window blinds' and two handles in the middle. These are used to change the shape of text boxes.

4 Make sure that pointer tool is selected and is shown as reverse video (black for white and vice versa). POINT the mouse on to the text, well away from any of the handles. Now CLICK and (keeping the left-hand mouse button held down) DRAG your text up to the top of the page.

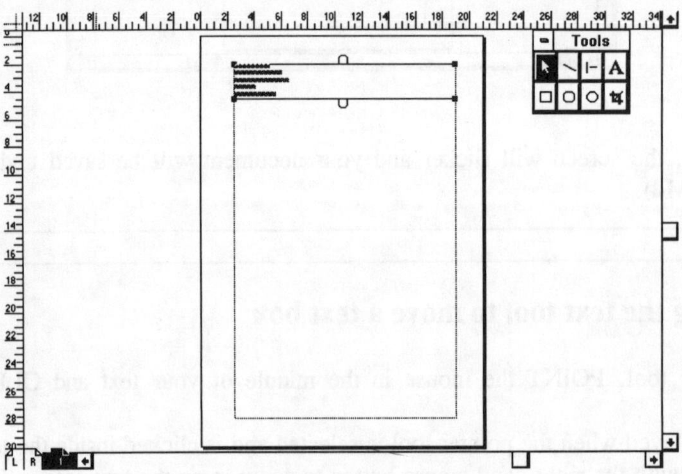

5 POINT the mouse at one of the two handles on the right side of the text box and then CLICK AND DRAG that handle towards the left until you reach the text. Release the mouse button.

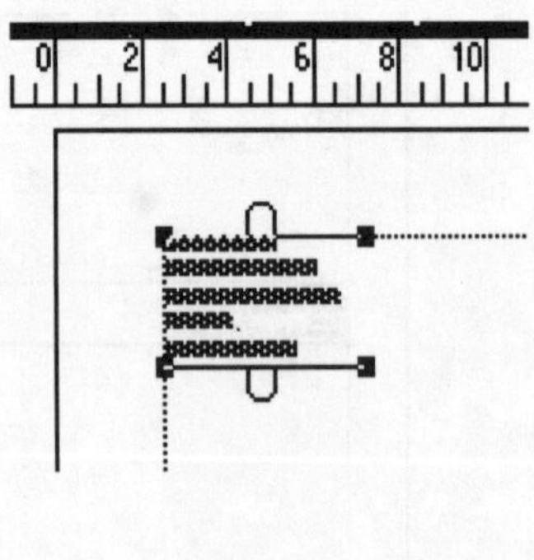

6 POINT the mouse on to the text, away from any of the handles. CLICK AND DRAG your text to the centre of the top of the page. *(Do not worry about accuracy for the moment).*

7 POINT the mouse on to the text and zoom in with the right-hand mouse button to see your text **Actual size**. CLICK the same button again to TOGGLE back to **Fit in window**. Notice that the text box has now disappeared.

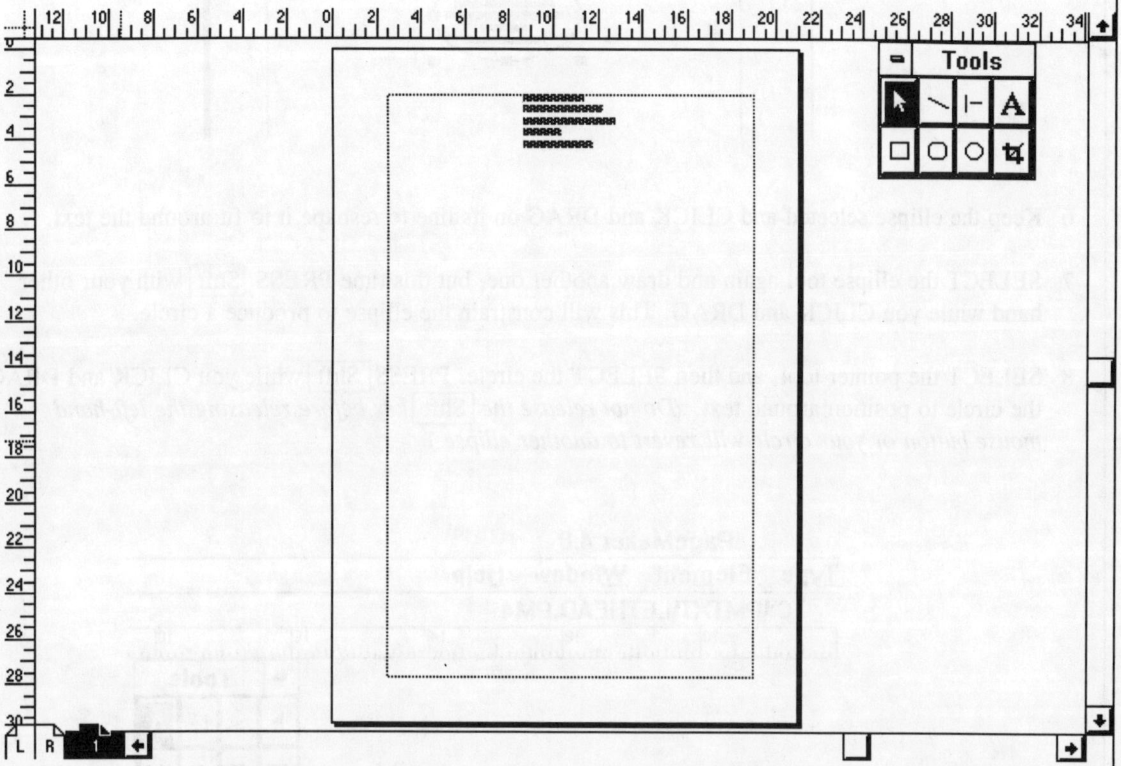

Activity 3.3 **Drawing an ellipse**

1 POINT the mouse on to your text and zoom in.

2 SELECT the ellipse tool.

3 POINT the mouse to the left of the text, CLICK and DRAG to the right to draw an ellipse. *(The thickness of the line will depend on the default already set.)*

4 SELECT the pointer tool. This is important. You cannot select, resize, reposition or delete a graphic unless the pointer tool is selected. The graphic drawing tools will only ever draw *new* graphics. They will not change ones already drawn.

5 SELECT the ellipse by clicking on its line (not inside). CLICK and DRAG *inside* the ellipse to reposition it around your text.

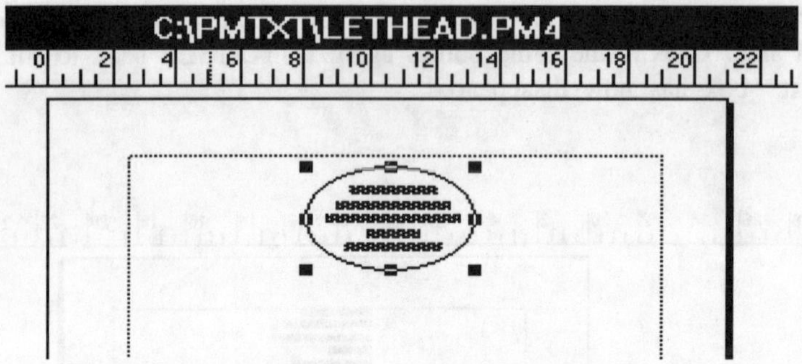

6 Keep the ellipse selected and CLICK and DRAG on its line to reshape it to fit around the text.

7 SELECT the ellipse tool again and draw another one, but this time PRESS [Shft] with your other hand while you CLICK and DRAG. This will constrain the ellipse to produce a circle.

8 SELECT the pointer tool, and then SELECT the circle. PRESS [Shft] while you CLICK and DRAG the circle to position around text. *(Do not release the [Shft] key before releasing the left-hand mouse button or your circle will revert to another ellipse.)*

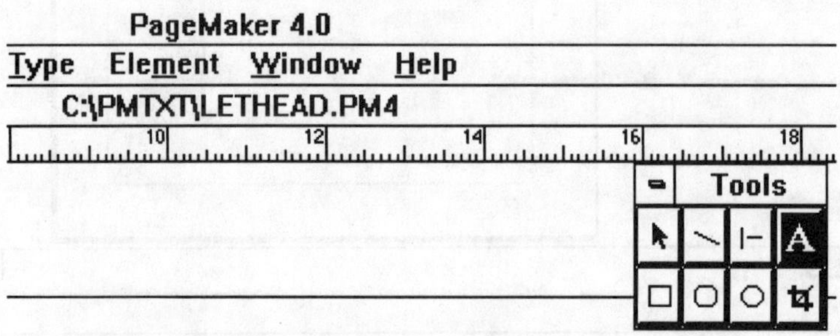

9 You can experiment with line widths using the **Element, line** menu (as in the example above). When you are satisified with your results, SAVE your document as LETHEAD.

Task 4 Simple text formatting

➢ In this task you will learn the basic technique of setting a typeface

Formatting text is one of the main jobs for any dtp program, and PM4 gives you lots of choices as to how your text will look.

For the moment you will only do the simplest formatting tasks: changing the typeface of a piece of text, altering its **style**, **size** and **alignment**. The **font** determines the typeface and look of your text, the **style** can be plain, bold, italics etc, the **size** depends on what job the text is doing, and the **alignment** places the text on the left, centre, right or justified from left to right of the paragraph margins.

Remember that you must always select something — in this case text — before you can make any changes to it, and you must select the text tool first if you are going to be working on text in the layout view.

Once your text is selected you format it with commands under the **Type menu** on the **Main menu bar**.

Activity 4.1 Applying a font to selected text

1 SELECT the text tool and then zoom into text if not already in **Actual size**.

2 POINT the mouse in front of the first character on the first line and CLICK. The screen pointer will turn into a blinking cursor.

3 CLICK AND DRAG across the first line of text so that the whole line appears in reverse video (black on white).

4 POINT the mouse at **Type** on the **Menu bar** and CLICK. The **Type menu** will be displayed. The selected text will remain in reverse video.

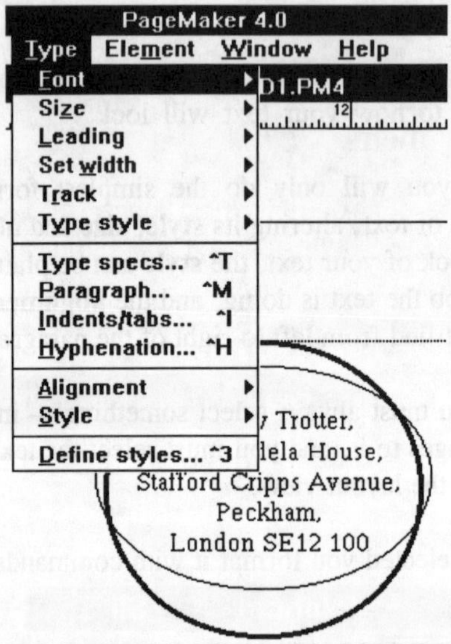

5 POINT the mouse at **Font** on the first line and CLICK. The **Font** sub-menu appears.

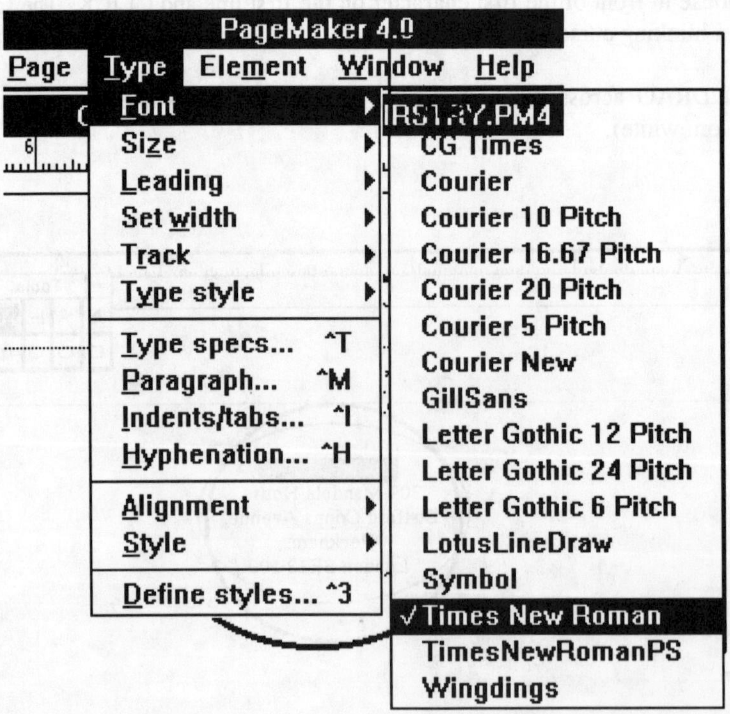

CLICK on Times (New Roman). This font will be selected as the typeface and applied to the first line of text which you selected earlier. *(If it already has a tick mark against it, that means it has already been selected as the PM4 default.)*

Activity 4.2 **Using the style menu**

1 SELECT the text tool and first line of text (if it is no longer selected). POINT the mouse on **Type**, CLICK and then SELECT **Type style** to open the sub-menu.

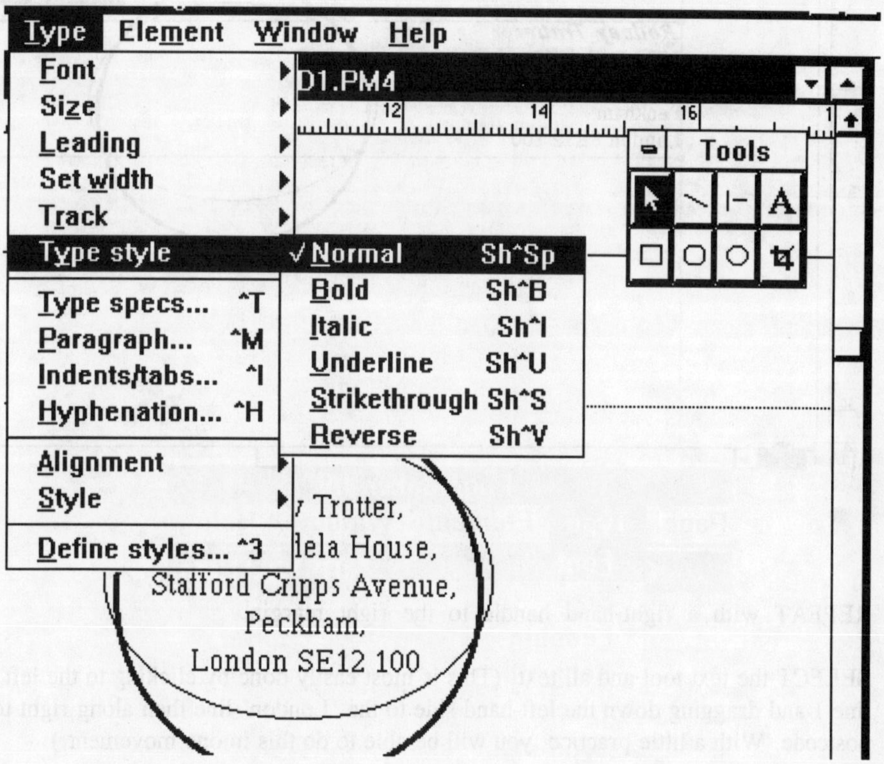

2 CLICK on **Italic** in the sub-menu. (**Normal** is the default if it has a check mark to the left.)

3 CLICK the mouse elsewhere on the page to deselect text. *Note* changes.

4 REPEAT the operation with **Type style, Bold**. Do not forget to SELECT your text first. Note also the PM4 keyboard shortcuts for text formatting: Shft + Ctrl + B for **Bold**, Shft + Ctrl + U for **Underline** etc.

5 DESELECT your text and *note* the results.

Activity 4.3 Setting text alignment

1 SELECT the pointer tool and then your text box. *(You should only have one on your page.)*

2 CLICK AND DRAG on a left-hand handle to bring text over to the left margin.

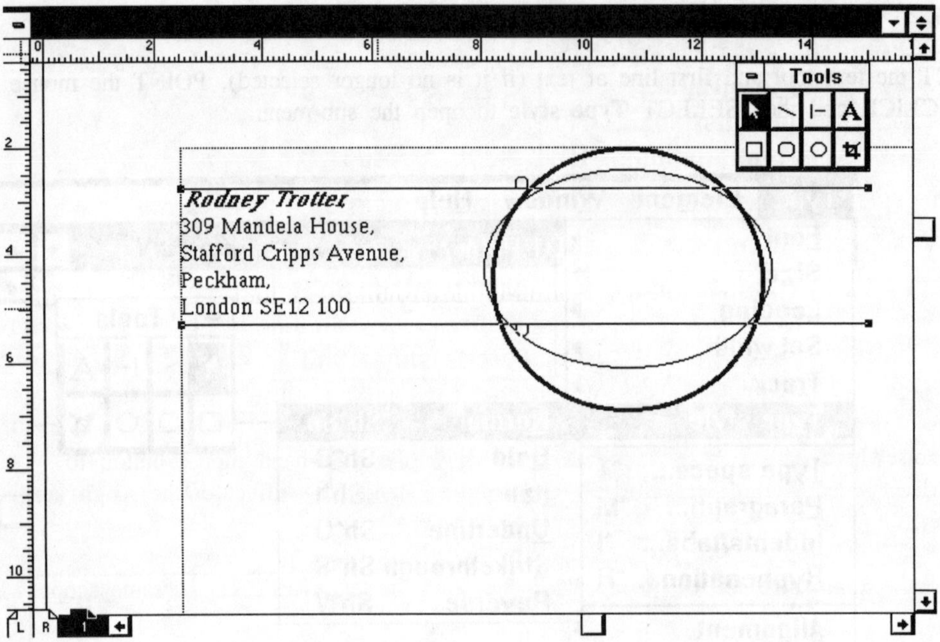

REPEAT with a right-hand handle to the right margin.

3 SELECT the text tool and all text. (This is most easily done by clicking to the left of 'Rodney' on line 1 and dragging down the left-hand side to the 'London' line then along right to the end of the postcode. With a little practice, you will be able to do this in one movement.)

4 POINT the mouse on **Type** and CLICK. SELECT **Alignment** to open another sub-menu.

5 CLICK on **Align centre**, and *note* the PM4 keyboard shortcut Shft + Ctrl + C .

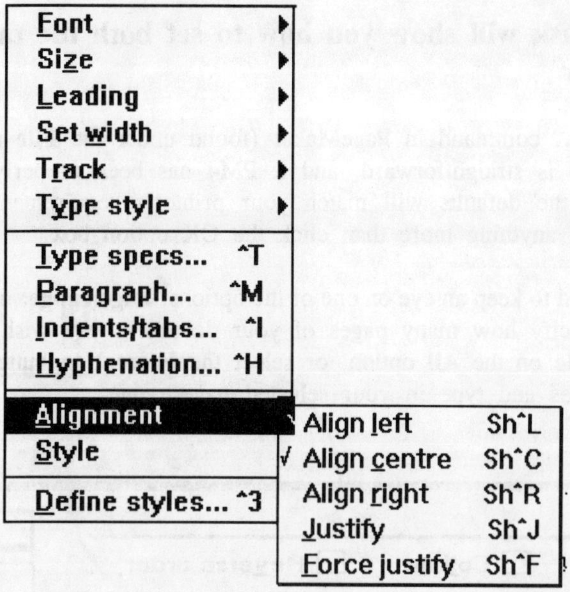

6 CLICK elsewhere on the page to deselect text. Use the right-hand mouse button to TOGGLE between **Actual size** and **Fit in window** and *note* the effect of the **Align centre** command.

7 SELECT the ellipse and DRAG to reposition it around the text. REPEAT the same action with the circle.

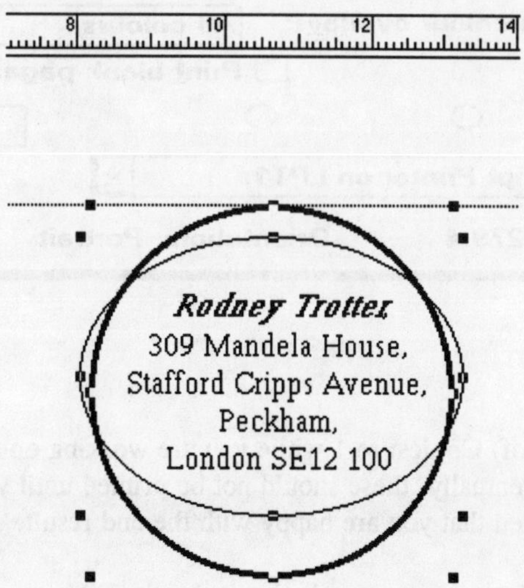

8 SELECT **File, Save as** and SAVE the document as **LETHEAD1**.

Task 5 Printing a document

➢This task will show you how to set both the target and current printer

The **Print...** command in PageMaker (found under the **File menu** on the **Main menu bar**) is straightforward, and if PM4 has been properly installed in Windows, the defaults will match your printer's requirements, and you will not need to do anything more than click the OK option box.

You do need to keep an eye on one of the options, **Page range:**, however. This allows you to specify how many pages of your document you wish to print: you can either toggle on the **All** option, or select the **From \ to** button and tab to the option boxes and type in your selected page range.

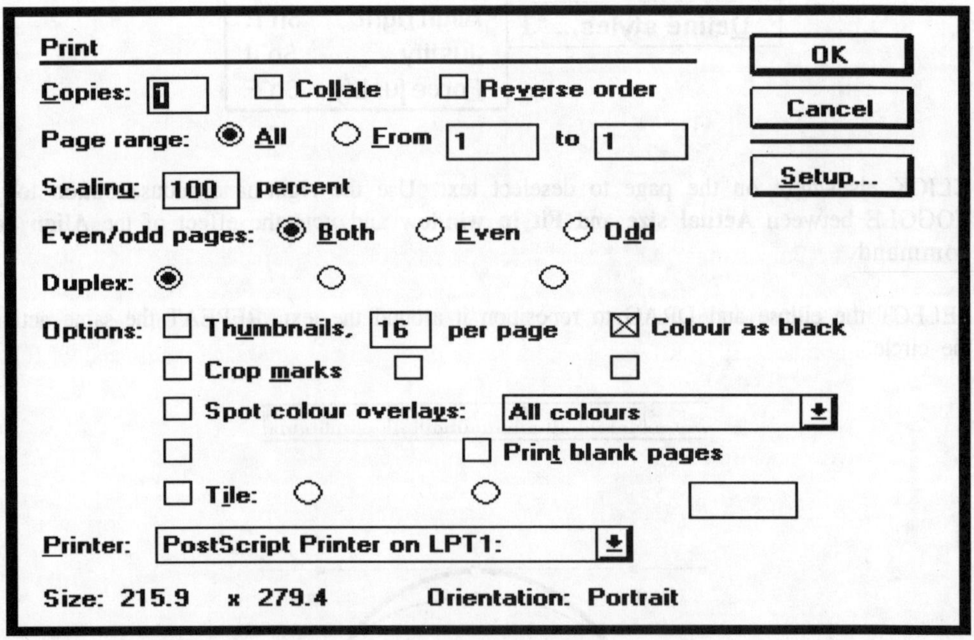

Keep (number of) **Copies:** to 1 while you are working on a job. Even if multiple copies are required eventually, these should not be printed until you have proof-read and carefully checked that you are happy with the end result.

The **Target printer...** command, also under the **File menu**, is used to organise your document to fit the printer on which it will finally be printed. If you know that you will printing the document in drafts and proofs on one printer with final output on another, higher quality, printer use the **Target printer...** command before you start work on the document, and set your current printer in the Printer: option box of the Print... dialogue box. For more information about this, *see* your PageMaker manual.

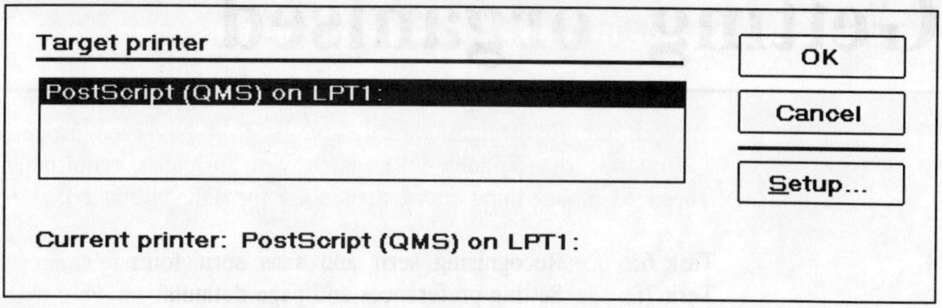

Activity 5.1 Printing a document

1 OPEN your **LETHEAD1** document if it is not still displayed on screen.

2 SELECT **File, Print.**

3 SELECT the **Page range: All** option button (if it is not set as default).

4 Check that the Printer: option box has the name of your current printer displayed, and if not, CLICK in the box, SCROLL through the list of printers until you reach yours, and CLICK on the

name to select it. The new printer type will appear in the option box.

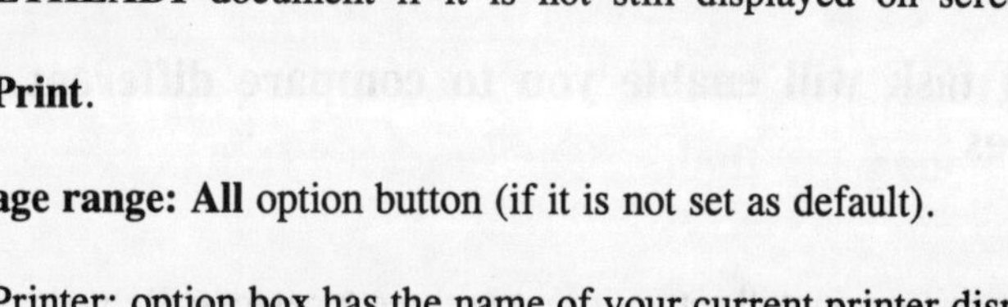

5 POINT the mouse at the OK option box and CLICK.
6 CLOSE **LETHEAD1.**

Section B

Getting organised

Task 6:	Recognising serif and sans serif fonts
Task 7:	Setting preferences and page defaults
Task 8:	Master pages and Insert/Remove pages
Task 9:	Measurements and rulers
Task 10:	Undo and Revert
Task 11:	Using the clipboard

Task 6 Recognising serif and sans serif fonts

➢ This task will enable you to compare different fonts and type styles

In this exercise you will set your text in three typefaces; Helvetica, Times New Roman and Wingdings; all of which are common fonts that should be available on your system. A font is a particular design of type, which comes in a variety of styles (roman or plain, bold, italic etc) and a variety of sizes. Many fonts have special purposes and a face which works well as a header may be very hard to read if used as body text.

Type size is usually measured in points, with 72 points to the inch. But because character width, kerning (space between the letters) and leading (space between the lines) depend on how the type has been designed, type in one font point size (typically 10) rarely covers the same area as the same point size in a different font. This can make layout much more complicated. Beware also if you have a range of fonts from different manufacturers, since even the most common fonts like Helvetica or Times may come in several versions which look slightly different and take up varying amounts of space on the page.

Helvetica is a sans serif typeface, Times New Roman is a serif face. Serifs are the little tails on the tips of the characters' horizontal and vertical strokes. They help to make serif faces look dignified, solid and unhurried. Compare the examples on page 24.

Sans serif types are designed to be bold and easy to read, and economical with space on the paper. Sans serif is often used for hard information, such as instructions. It is common to have sans serif headlines and serif body text - *The* **Guardian** newspaper uses a combination of both to make up its masthead (*title*).

Activity 6.1 **Inputting and copying text**

1 OPEN **File, New....**

2 SELECT the text tool.

3 TYPE in a company name, and address. PRESS Enter at the end of each line.

4 PRESS Ctrl + A . This will select all text. SELECT **Edit, Copy**.

5 CLICK to place the cursor after the last line of the address. SELECT **Edit, Paste**.

6 REPEAT twice. This will give you four blocks of text which you can format to different specifications.

Activity 6.2 **Formatting text**

1 PLACE the cursor at the beginning of the text. DRAG over the first three lines to select the first copy of the address.

2 SELECT **Type, Font** and CLICK to open font window. CLICK on Helvetica to SELECT.

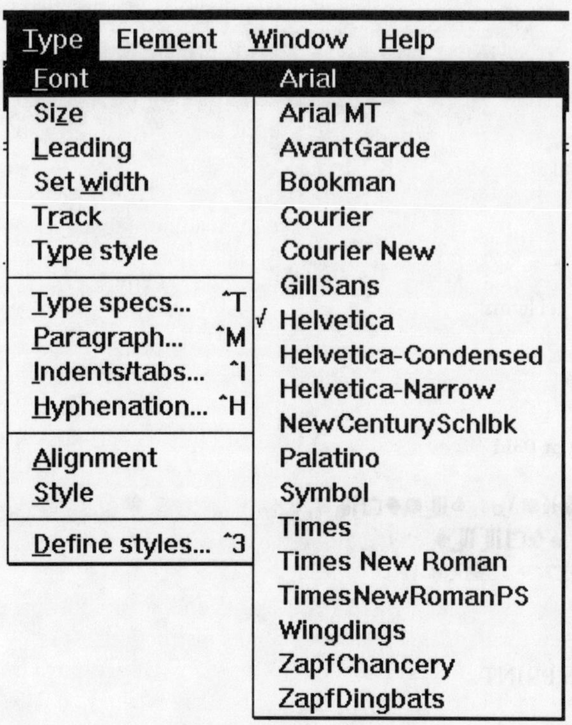

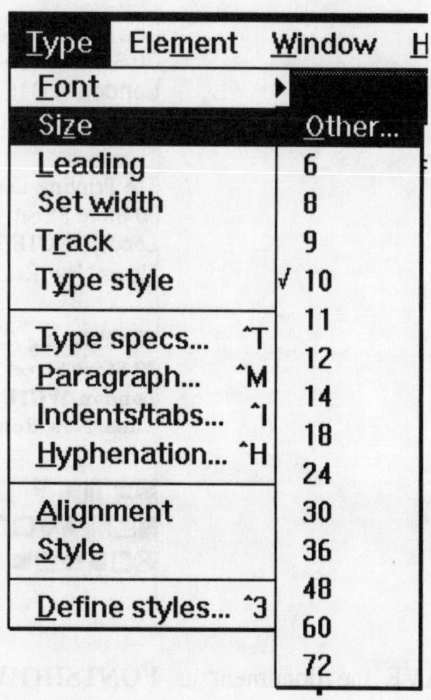

3 SELECT **Type, Size** and SELECT 10 points.

4 PLACE the cursor after the third line of text.

5 TYPE **Helvetica 10 pt Normal**.

6 REPEAT steps 1-4 in the second text block but this time SELECT Times New Roman.

7 TYPE **Times New Roman 10 pt Normal**.

Activity 6.3 Using bold typestyle and Wingdings

1 SELECT the third text block and FORMAT as for the second text block but TYPE *Times New Roman 10 pt Bold*.

2 SELECT **Type, Type style** and SCROLL to select Bold. (Remember that the text must be selected first.)

3 SELECT the fourth text block and FORMAT the text as 12 point Wingdings.

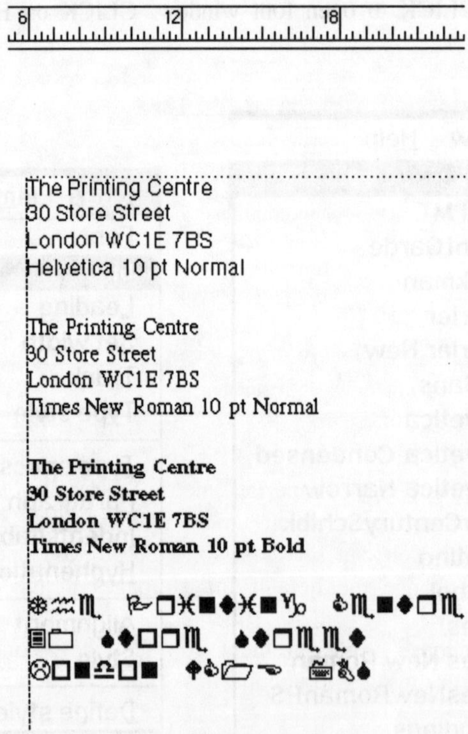

4 SAVE the document as **FONTSHOW** and PRINT.

Task 7 Setting preferences and page defaults

➢ This task will enable you to set measurements for your document

PageMaker is one of the easiest dtp programs to learn. However, even with PageMaker, you need to know the basic size and layout of the page before you start. Although an acceptable format may have already been set in PM4's defaults on the machine you are using, you may be asked to change these in order to undertake the exercises in this *Guide*.

There are three main places where many of the defaults are set in PM4: the **Edit, Preferences...** and the **File, Page setup...** dialogue boxes, as well as the **Master pages** of any document you are working on. It is wise to avoid changing defaults once you have started working on your document. Sometimes such changes are unavoidable, but they almost always create a lot of extra work.

The **Edit, Preferences...** command gives options on quite a wide range of defaults, but for the moment you are just going to set metric measurements with it.

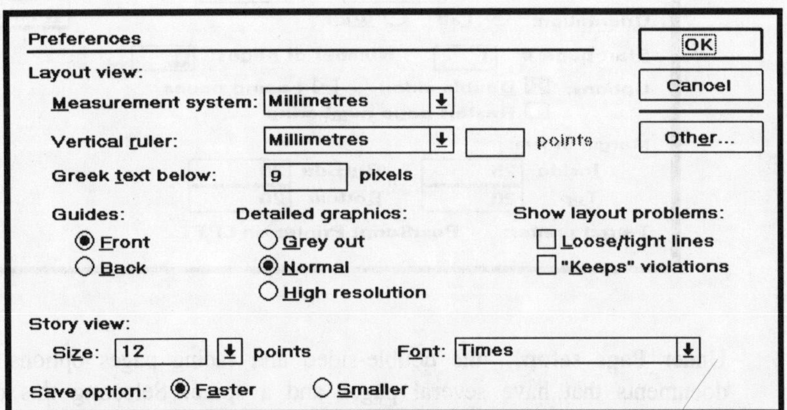

The measurement units (imperial, metric, picas etc) that you use for margins, and all the other measurement units in other options, are set under **Edit, Preferences...**. You can set these units before you open or create a new document to change the default for all pages in the document.

In general, choose a measurement you feel most comfortable with. (*Note* that metric units are used throughout this *Guide*.)

You have already seen the **Page setup...** dialogue box which appears automatically when you use **File, New...** to open a new document. It controls the most basic choices about any document: page size, whether it is to be single or double sided, and what size the margins are between the type and the edge of the paper.

If Windows has been set up properly on your machine, the paper size loaded into your printer will be the default shown by PageMaker. This *Guide* assumes that A4-sized paper is available. Maximum page size, which will be either A3 or A4, is usually determined by your printer. You can also print smaller sizes, such as A5 (the usual size of a paperback book).

To fit two small pages on to a larger page on your printer, you need to set up your document on a larger page size and divide it in two before you start laying it out (e.g. an A4 landscape page split in half will produce two A5 portrait pages). *See* your PageMaker manual for more information about booklet preparation.

Page setup... is where you set your margins. Make sure your margins are not too small and remember that copy crammed onto the page is difficult to read. If you are producing a book-type layout you should leave enough room in the centre margins along the spine for the document to be bound and perhaps trimmed with a guillotine. Typically, margins for an A4 document might be as follows:

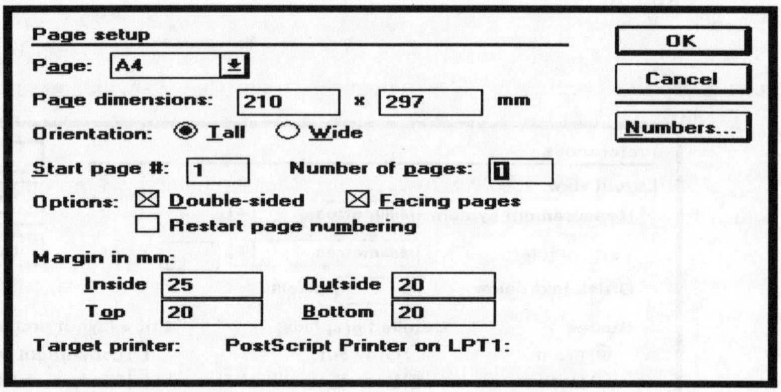

Under **Page setup...** the double-sided and facing pages options are used for documents that have several pages and a spine. Selecting this option gives you left-hand and right-hand pages which will display on your screen as a double page spread. You do not need to check facing pages if you are producing single sheets. Letter-type layouts, for example, are generally only typed or printed on one side of the paper.

The L and R double page spread icon at the bottom left corner of your PM4 screen allows you to open the **Master pages** of your document by clicking on it. These **Master pages** are used to set symmetrical margins, column guides, guides across facing pages, and page numbers in the outside margins for book-style layouts which are double-sided (printed on both sides of the paper). Whatever formatting is set on the **Master pages** refers only to that document, not to all your documents.

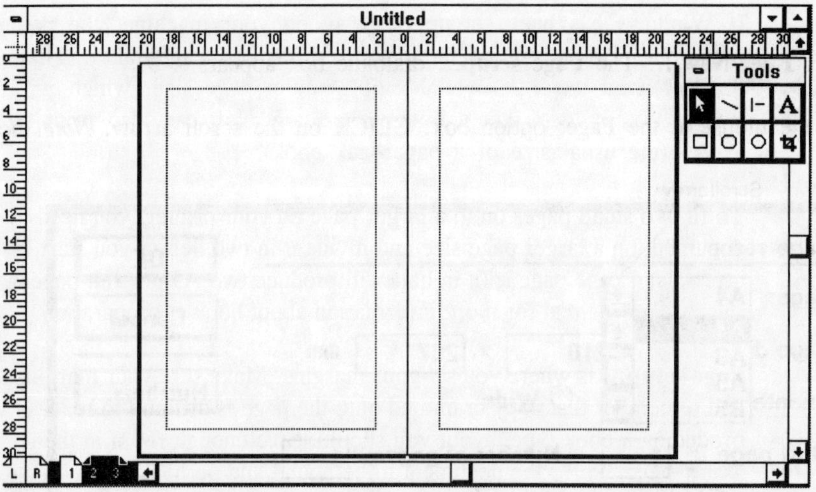

Activity 7.1 Setting metric rulers

1 SELECT **Edit, Preferences....** The dialogue box on page 25 will appear, although it may have different (default) settings.

2 POINT the mouse at the scroll arrow on the Measurement system: option box and CLICK. The following choice of measurement units will appear.

3 SELECT Millimetres.

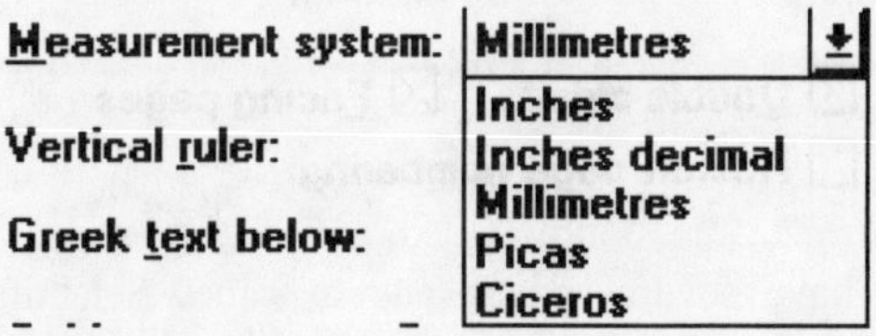

4 REPEAT this action in the Vertical ruler: option box below.

5 CLICK on OK.

Activity 7.2 Opening the Page setup dialogue box for a new document

1 SELECT **File, New....** The **Page setup...** dialogue box appears.

2 POINT the mouse at the Page: option box. CLICK on the scroll arrow. *Note* the choice of

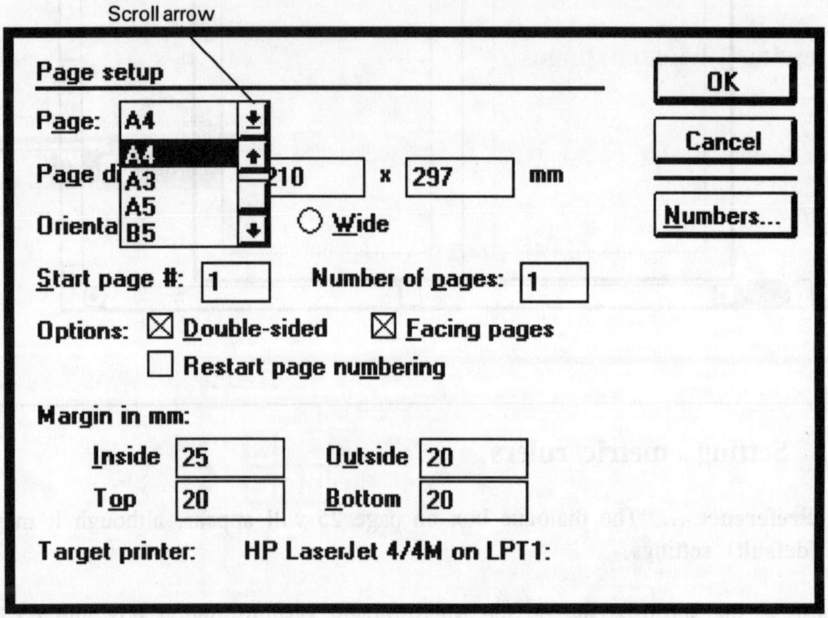

page sizes available. SELECT A4 (if it is not set as default).

3 POINT the mouse at Options: and CLICK in both the Double-sided and Facing pages

boxes. Do not CLICK in either box if it is already checked (crossed). This means that these options have already been set in default.

4 DOUBLE CLICK in the Inside: option box under the Margin in mm: option, so that the figure in the box is highlighted.

5 TYPE **20**.

6 TAB to the Outside: option box. TYPE **20**.

7 REPEAT these actions in the Top: and Bottom: option boxes.

8 PRESS Enter . The first page of a new document will appear on screen.

Activity 7.3 Viewing Master pages

1 POINT the mouse at the **Master page** icon in the bottom left-hand corner of PM4's window.

2 CLICK and the left- and right-hand **Master pages** will appear on screen.

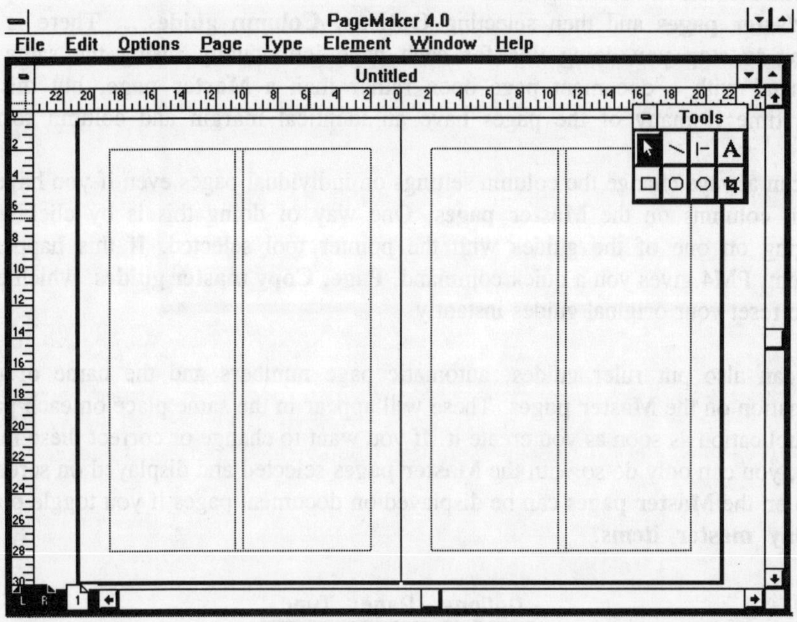

The number of columns (indicated by dotted, parallel vertical lines) depends on the default set by **Options, Column guides....** Here, it is two columns per page.

Task 8 Master pages and Insert/Remove pages

➢ **This task will show you how to set up columns and default items using the Master pages and how to insert and remove pages**

Master pages are an extremely useful aspect of the PageMaker program. They are used for placing items which recur throughout an entire document – headers, footers, column guides, page numbers etc. They should not be used for positioning text or images, unless these are to be repeated in the same position throughout the document.

Usually, when starting a new document, the **Master pages** are set up first, and after all recurring items have been positioned correctly, page 1 is opened and text and/or illustrations laid out on the document pages.

You can set default column guides for the whole publication by selecting and opening the **Master pages** and then selecting **Options, Column guides...**. There is nothing to stop you doing this for each page individually, using the same command with a document page open rather than a **Master page**, but this can waste time if many of the pages have an identical margin and column format.

You can always change the column settings on individual pages even if you have default columns on the **Master pages**. One way of doing this is by clicking and dragging on one of the guides with the pointer tool selected. If this happens by accident, PM4 gives you a quick command, **Page, Copy master guides**, which enables you to reset your original guides instantly.

You can also put ruler guides, automatic page numbers and the name of the publication on the **Master pages**. These will appear in the same place on each page of the publication as soon as you create it. If you want to change or correct these master items, you can only do so with the **Master pages** selected and displayed on screen. Items on the **Master pages** can be displayed on document pages if you toggle on **Page, Display master items**.

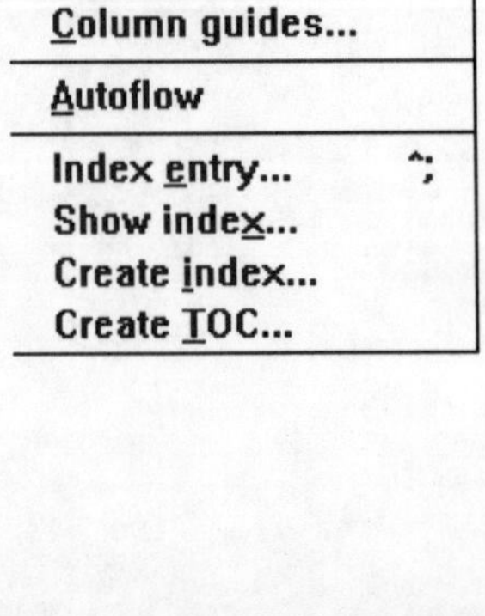

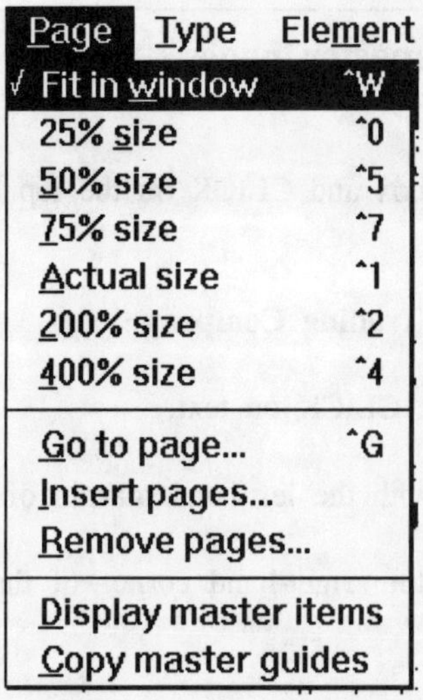

Activity 8.1 Setting columns on master pages

1 OPEN **Master pages** of your **FONTSHOW** document (*see* Activity 7.3.)

2 SELECT **Options, Column guides….**

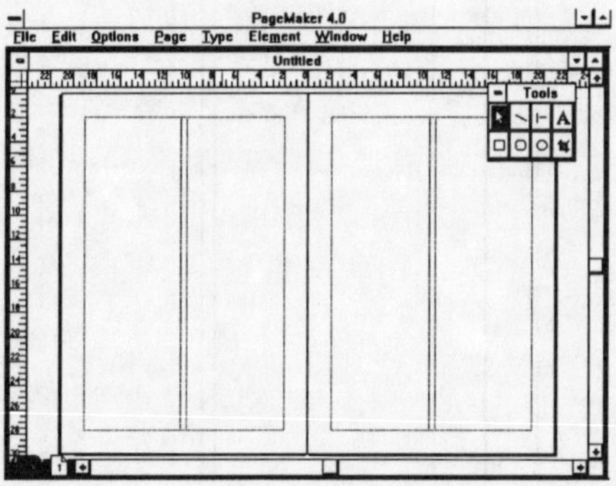

3 DOUBLE CLICK the contents of the Number of columns: option box to highlight it.

4 TYPE **2.**

5 TAB to the Space between columns: box. TYPE in **5** mm (usual default). CLICK on OK.

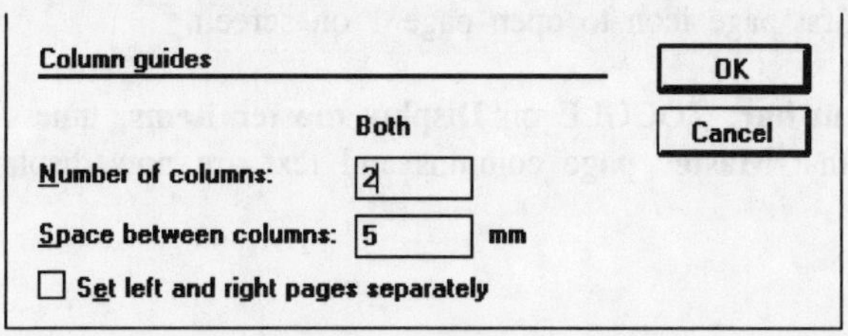

Activity 8.2 Placing text on master pages

1 SELECT the text tool in the Toolbox and CLICK on the top left-hand corner of the left-hand page to place the cursor.

2 TYPE in **Trotter's International Trading Company**.

3 SELECT the pointer tool and then CLICK on text.

4 MOVE the text so that it aligns with the left-hand margin of the page.

5 REPEAT these actions in the bottom right-hand corner of the right page.

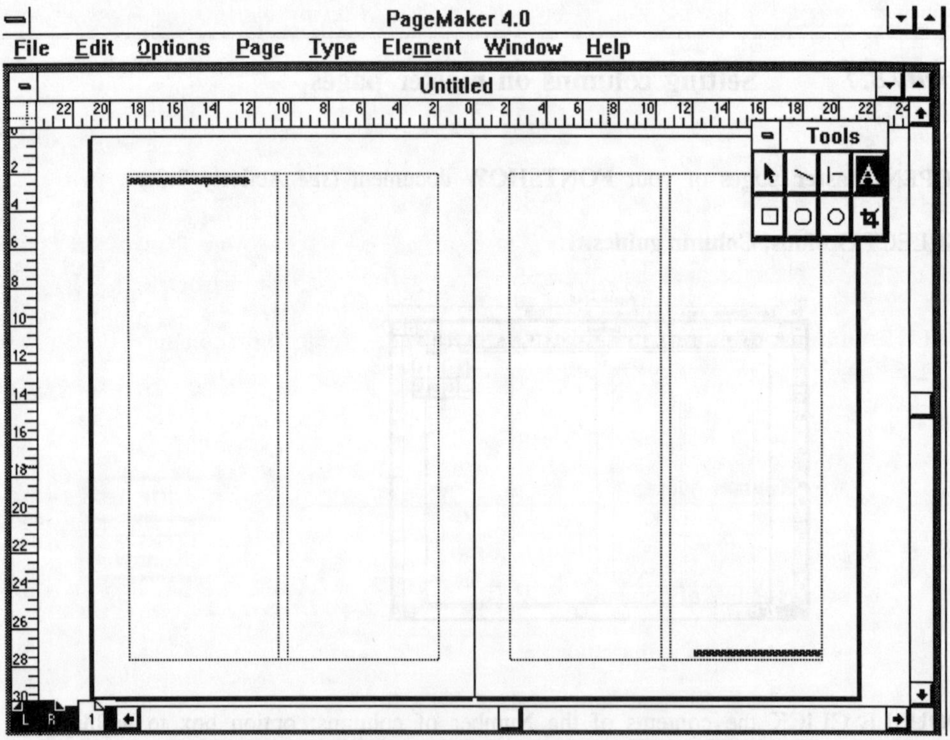

Activity 8.3 Creating new pages

1 DOUBLE CLICK on the first page icon to open page 1 on screen.

2 SELECT **Page** on the **Menu bar**. TOGGLE on **Display master items**, unless it is already checked by default. *Note* that **Master page** columns and text are now displayed on a document page.

3 CLICK on the text. Nothing will happen. Master items can only be selected and changed if the **Master pages** are open on screen.

4 SELECT **Page, Insert pages.**

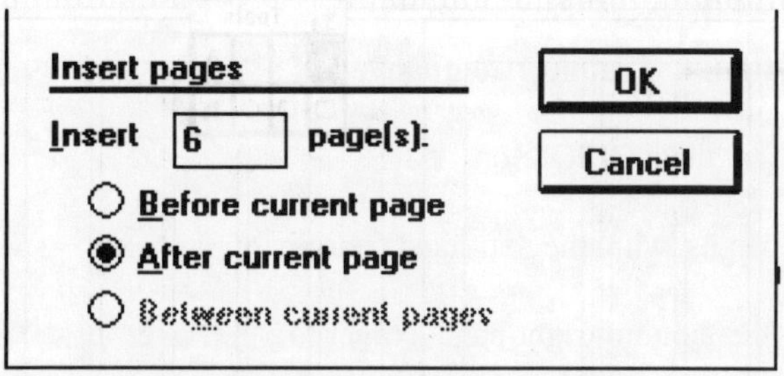

5 DOUBLE CLICK in the Insert page[s]: option box and TYPE **6**. Document icons now look like this.

6 DOUBLE CLICK on the icon of page 6 to display it on screen. *Note* that master columns and text have been created automatically.

7 SELECT **Options, Column guides.** HIGHLIGHT the Number of columns: option box and TYPE **5**.

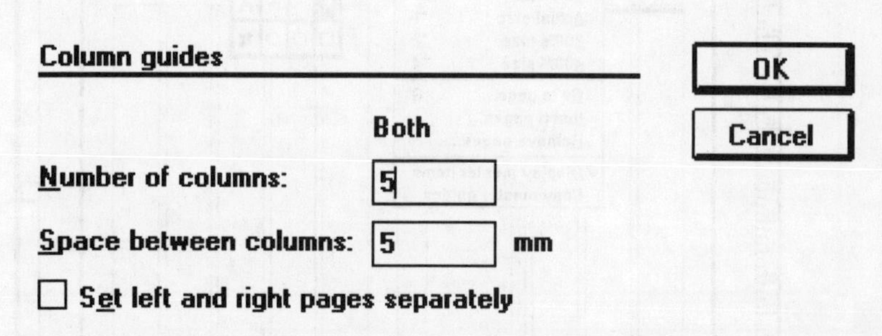

8 POINT the mouse at one of the column guides on the left-hand page (page 5). CLICK AND DRAG one of the column guides into a new position.

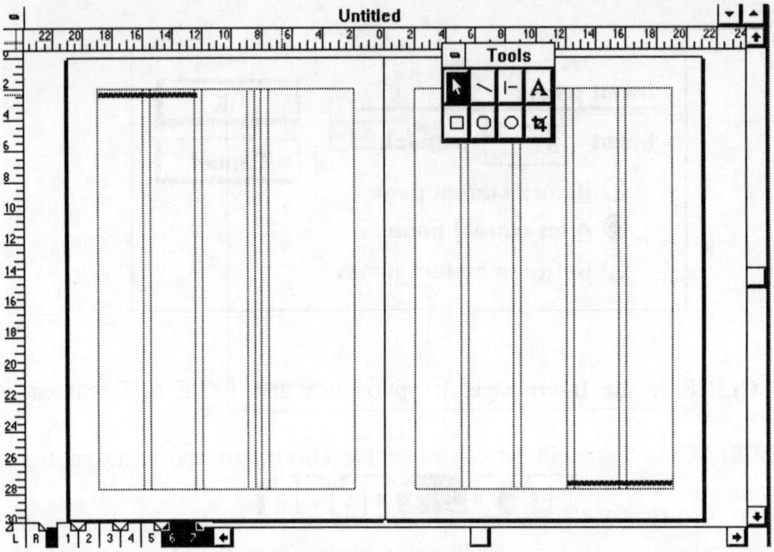

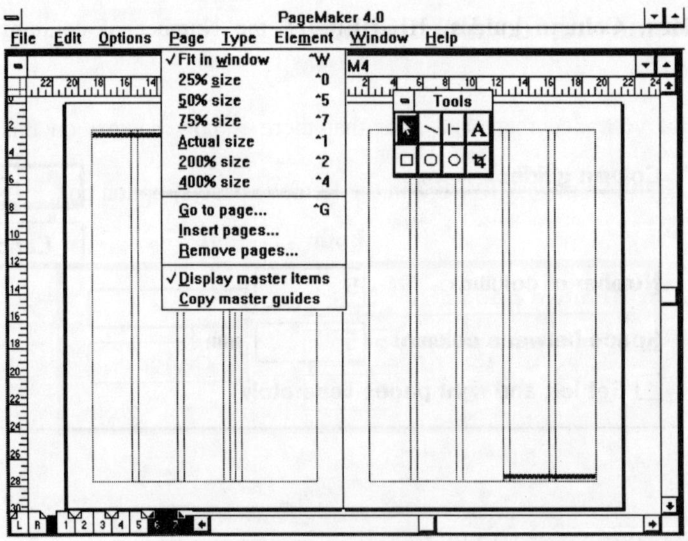

9 SELECT **Page, Copy master guides**. *Note* that the column guides on page 5 have reverted to the same configuration as the **Master page**.

Activity 8.4 Rescuing text entered on Master page

1 OPEN **Master pages**. SELECT the pointer tool and then **Edit, Select all**. Note the keyboard shortcut ^A (Ctrl + A).

2 SELECT **Edit, Cut**. Text will be copied to the **Clipboard** and removed from **Master pages**.

3 OPEN page 2. SELECT **Edit, Paste**. CLICK AND DRAG the text into the correct position. This is the procedure to use if you accidentally enter text on the **Master pages** instead of a document page.

Activity 8.5 Removing document pages

1 OPEN page 1 of your document and *note* that there is now no text on this page.

2 SELECT **Page, Remove pages**. TYPE **2** in the Remove page[s] option box.

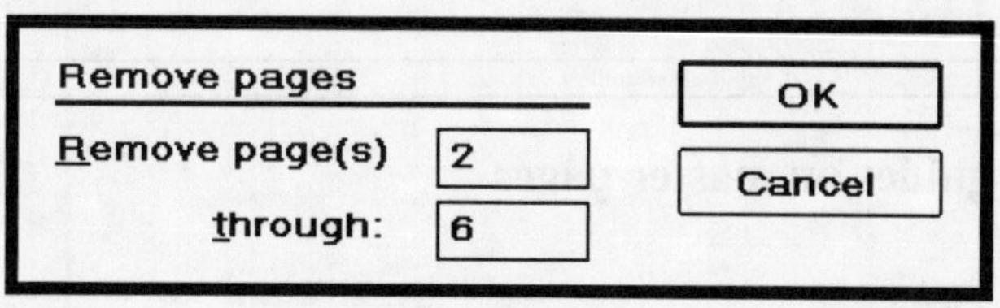

3 TAB to through: option box and TYPE **6**.

4 PRESS Enter and *note* change in document icons.

Be careful: the default page numbers for **Remove pages** are always those open on screen.

Task 9

Measurements and rulers

➢ This task demonstrates how to display rulers and set guides on all pages

PM4 can display rulers along the top and left side of any page on screen. These rulers will not print out and can be hidden to save space on small screens. By clicking and dragging these rulers you can create horizontal or vertical guides anywhere on the page. If a guide is placed on a (left- or right-hand) **Master page**, it will be displayed on all (left- or right-hand) document pages. If you toggle off the Facing pages option, a **Master page** guide will appear on all document pages.

Documents look much more professional if lines of type are aligned symmetrically, and this is one of the things that the guides are used for.

A floating marker in the horizontal or vertical ruler can be used to measure guide placement. Whatever size you view your document, the rulers' measurement units will change in the same proportion.

Activity 9.1 Displaying and hiding rulers

1 OPEN **Master pages** of a new document and *note* whether the document on screen is displaying horizontal and vertical rulers along the top and left-hand side of the PM4 window.

2 SELECT **Options, Rulers**. If rulers are not displayed by default, TOGGLE on.

3 *Note* the measurement units on the rulers then SELECT **Page, 200%** size. *Note* that the ruler measurements have been magnified by a factor of two.

4 SELECT **Page, Fit in window**.

Activity 9.2 Place guides on master pages

1 OPEN **Master pages** and SELECT the pointer tool.

2 POINT the mouse at the horizontal ruler. CLICK AND DRAG to create a guide below the bottom edge of the margin.

3 TOGGLE on **Page, Display master items**, and OPEN a document page to see the guide.

Task 10 Undo and Revert

➢This task will teach you some rapid ways to recover from mistakes

You may have already discovered that it is quite easy to make mistakes and forget commands in dtp, even in PageMaker. PM4 gives you a number of useful ways of coping with human error: **Undo**, **Revert**, and **Revert** to **mini-save**.

If you have forgotten what item was last copied, you can check by displaying the **Clipboard**. This is quicker than pasting on to the pasteboard (or a blank page) and then deleting the pasted item.

If you have made a mistake, always apply **Edit, Undo** [Ctrl + Z] *or* [Alt + Bksp] immediately. This only works for your last action and does not work with a number of text and graphics options, but it can be a life-saver if, for example, you have accidentally deleted part of a layout that has taken a lot of time to create and you have also forgotten to save it recently.

Dtp is a complicated procedure and everybody at some time finds that they have created a mess they cannot sort out. If you save frequently, as you should, you can use the **File, Revert** command to take you back to the last version you saved.

Most users forget to save as often as they should. PM4 will often remember to save your document for you by creating a mini-save automatically. Mini-saves are triggered by a number of actions including moving to another page, inserting or deleting a page, and printing or copying (using the **Clipboard**).

Since there might be a danger that you wanted your last saved version rather than a more recent mini-save, you can only bring back the last mini-saved version of your document by holding down the [Shft] key when you select **File, Revert**.

Activity 10.1 Using Undo to correct a mistake

1 OPEN **LETHEAD1**.

2 With the pointer tool selected, SELECT any item on the page.

3 PRESS [Del]. The selected item will be deleted.

4 SELECT **Edit, Undo**. The item will be restored.

Activity 10.2 Reverting to last saved version of file

1 SELECT another item on the page in **LETHEAD 1**.

2 DRAG the item into another position.

3 SELECT **File, Revert**. The current document will close and the previous version will be reopened.

Activity 10.3 Activating and reverting to a mini-save

1 REPEAT actions 10.2.1 and 10.2.2.

2 CLICK on a page icon (remember this is in the bottom left-hand corner of the screen and has a 1 on it). This will activate a mini-save.

3 SELECT an item and PRESS the Del key.

4 PRESS the Shft key as you SELECT **File, Revert**. The last mini-saved version of the file will open.

5 SELECT **Edit, Revert**. Mini-save will close and the original version of the file will open.

6 SAVE AS **LETHEAD1** (again) to delete the mini-save version.

Task 11 Using the clipboard

➢This task will show you how to Display and Save the contents of the Copy/Cut/Paste commands

When you use the **Cut** or **Copy** commands, the selected item is stored in a Windows' file called a clipboard. You do not have to be able to see the clipboard window opened to use **Cut**, **Copy** or **Paste**, and often it would be a waste of screen space or work time to have it visible.

However, there may be times when you cannot remember if an item has been copied into the clipboard or not. Using the Windows' **Clipboard** command, you can not only display it, you can also save its contents to a separate file.

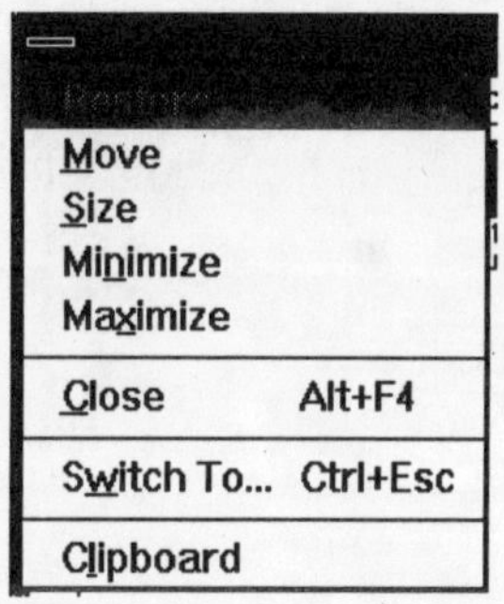

You will often create items, or groups of items, that you subsequently want to use again in another PM4 document. By copying such items to the clipboard and using **Clipboard, Save** you can reuse the same piece of work as often as you need to. This can save a lot of time.

To retrieve a clipboard file which has been saved previously, use the **Clipboard, Open** command. This is located in the Menu control box of the PM4 window. A clipboard file must have a **.CLP** tail and you can experiment with using it to transfer items into and out of other programs. Do not assume that items that you attempt to transfer this way will always be compatible with another program, but you should be able to use the clipboard with other programs published by Aldus.

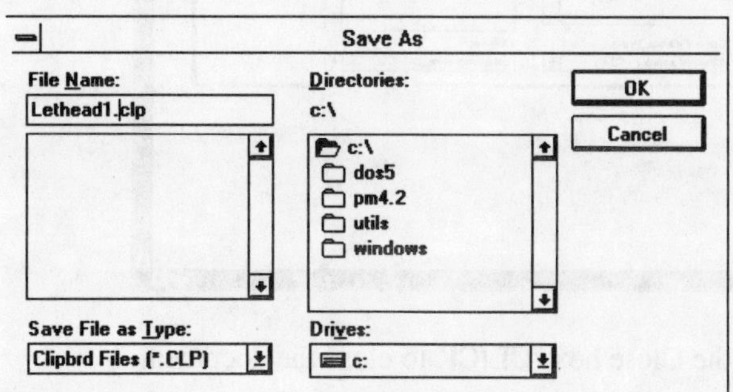

Activity 11.1 Viewing the clipboard

1 OPEN **LETHEAD1**.

2 With the pointer tool selected, SELECT **Edit, Select All**.

3 SELECT **Edit, Copy**.

4 POINT the mouse at the Menu control box in the top left-hand corner of PM4 (not the document) window.

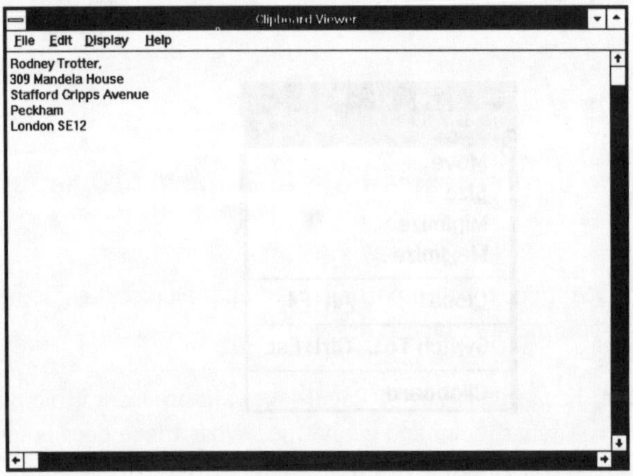

5 SCROLL to **Clipboard** and CLICK. The clipboard window will appear on screen.

6 SELECT **Save** on the **Clipboard menu bar**. SAVE AS **LETHEAD1.CLP**.

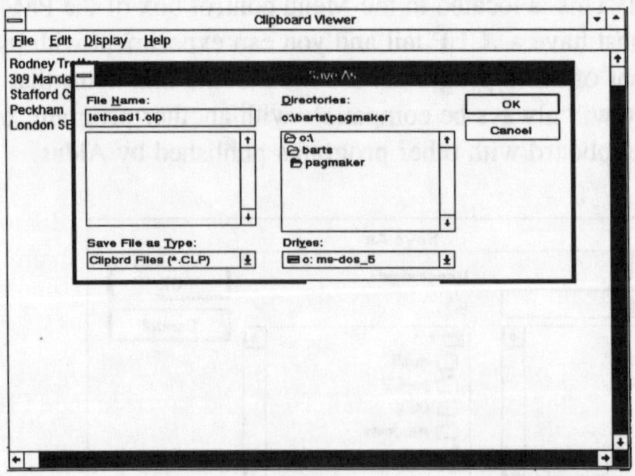

7 POINT the mouse at the Close box. CLICK to close the document.

Section C

Creating simple documents

Task 12 Placing an external file

➢This task demonstrates how to import text or a picture onto the page

PageMaker's technique of importing text and pictures on to the page is done with a single command: **Place** Ctrl + P.

This command lies at the heart of PageMaker and to use it effectively you need to feel comfortable with what it can and cannot do. What **Place** does is to open a file window to let you choose any file that you wish to import on to your page. The sequence goes: i) Select the pointer tool and then select **File, Place**. ii) click on the directory window in the Place dialogue box until the file you want appears. iii) Select the file you want by pointing and clicking. iv) Open the file. PM4 then returns you to your document with the text file or picture loaded on your screen pointer. Click anywhere on the page or pasteboard and the imported file will flow on to the page.

To make it easy PM4 keeps you informed about what is happening. In step iii) PageMaker will tell you if the file you have selected is a text or a picture file (because in the heat of composition it is easy to forget!). When you return to your document your screen pointer will change shape to show whether it is carrying a graphic or text. If you are importing text, this shape will also tell you how that text will flow on the page.

If you change your mind in mid-sequence, simply select the text tool and the imported material will be aborted. This will not harm the original file in any way, so you can always **Place** it again when you are ready.

The activities which follow require you to use the text and picture files listed in Appendices 1 & 2. Pictures can be scanned in and saved in the **.TIF** format. If you do not have access to a scanner use photocopies of the picture files. Prepare your text on your usual word processing file or type directly into the Story editor. If you have problems with the way text comes in, make sure that the correct import filter is installed under the Aldus Setup program.

If PageMaker does not recognise your word processing file, i.e. it fails to appear in the folder opened under **File, Place**, use the Windows' **Program manager** to

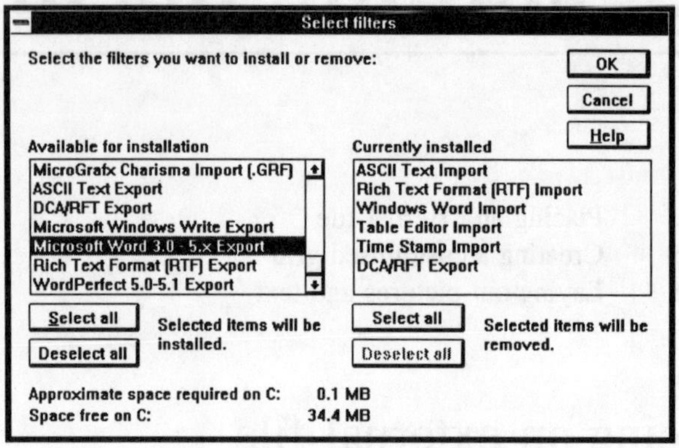

go back into your word processing file and save it as an ASCII file, with no carriage returns, or text only. You must give the file a **.TXT** tail. You will probably lose any formatting done on the word processor, except paragraph breaks, but PageMaker's **Place** command will always recognise an ASCII text file with the correct tail. If it still does not show up in the **Place** window, you are looking in the wrong folder (sub-directory).

If you want to fit text into a specific area, click and drag the mouse to move the screen pointer over the area on the layout where you want the text to go. You can do the same with pictures, clicking and dragging over the area where you want the picture to fall; but beware, this will distort the picture and give it new proportions. A distorted picture can be very effective, if it has been done deliberately. Accidental distortion simply looks like a mistake and may be difficult to print.

Below, is a list of cursor types and what they show. The first three symbols are 'window blind' handles which can tell you how text in a text box is running.

 Text box handle: more hidden text to come

 Text box handle: end of text

 Text box handle: more text exists in linked text box

 Screen pointer: text loaded and ready to place in column

 Screen pointer: autoflow text ready to place, will create new columns/pages as required by length of text

 Semi-automatic, text flows to end of column and this cursor reappears

 Cursor ready to place bitmapped or paint-type graphic

 Cursor loaded with object-orientated or draw-type graphic

 Cursor loaded with tiff-type picture such as a scan

 Cursor ready to place an EPS (Encapsulated PostScript format) graphic

Activity 12.1 Creating a two column layout with guides

1 OPEN **File, New....**

2 In the Page setup... dialogue box SET Page to A4 (if not set in default) and all margins to **20** mm.

3 DOUBLE CLICK on **Master pages** to open them.

4 SELECT **Options, Column guides....**

5 CLICK in the Number of columns: option box to select contents. TYPE in **2**.

6 TAB to Space between columns: and TYPE **10** mm.

7 DRAG a guide out of the horizontal ruler and SET it **50** mm below the margin at the top of the page.

8 DRAG four horizontal guides on to the page and set each at **50** mm below the one above.

9 Save as **BIZCARD**.

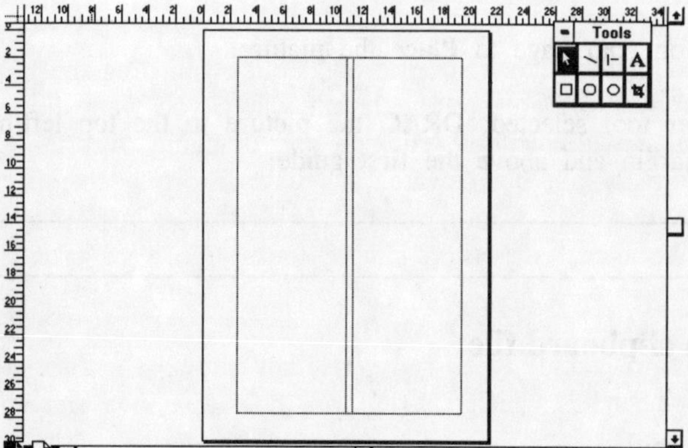

Activity 12.2 Placing a picture (tiff) file

1 CLICK on the first document page to open it. (Note that columns, margins and guides from the master page are displayed).

2 SELECT **File, Place.**

3 FIND the **LOGO.TIF** file in the sub-directory in which it has been stored. CLICK on the drive letters in the Files/Directories: box to change drives, and/or CLICK on [..] to open the root directory.

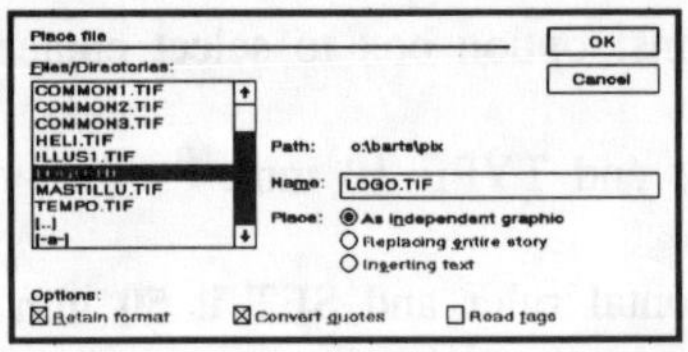

4 CLICK on the sub-directory to view its contents.

5 When the **LOGO.TIF** file appears, CLICK the screen pointer on it to select, then CLICK on OK. You will return to document view with the picture loaded into the screen pointer.

6 CLICK the Screen pointer on your page to **Place** the picture.

7 With the picture and pointer tool selected, DRAG the picture to the top left-hand corner of the page inside the top margin and above the first guide.

Activity 12.3 Pasting a clipboard file

1 OPEN the Control Menu box and SELECT **Clipboard**.

2 With a blank clipboard window displayed, SELECT **Open...** on the **Menu bar**.

3 SCROLL to the directory where **LETHEAD1.CLP** is stored and SELECT.

4 DOUBLE CLICK on the Control Menu box to close it. PRESS Shft + Ins to **Paste** the item.

5 CLICK to place text. CLICK AND DRAG the text into position.

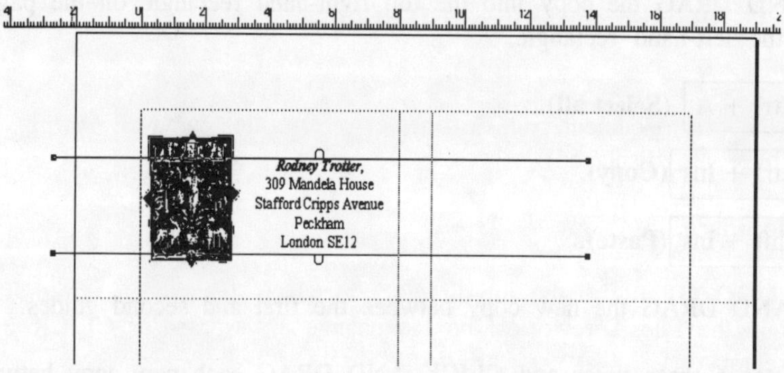

6 CLICK AND DRAG the text box handles to resize as necessary.

Activity 12.4 Using Select all and Copy

1 With the pointer tool selected, SELECT **Edit, Select all.**

2 SELECT **Edit, Copy**, then SELECT **Edit, Paste.**

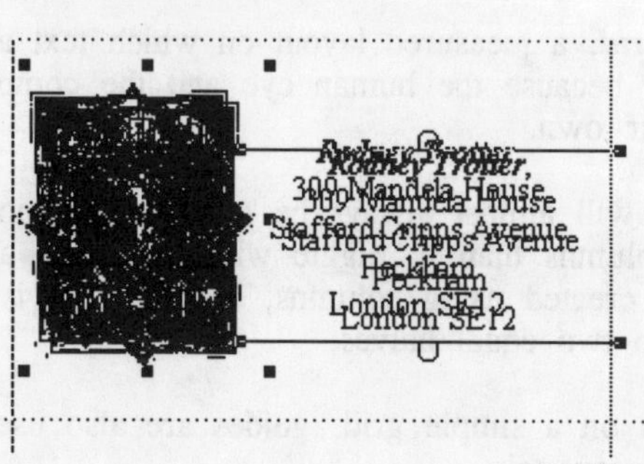

3 CLICK AND DRAG the copy into the top right-hand rectangle on the page and position it to match the left-hand rectangle.

4 PRESS Ctrl + A (**Select all**).

5 PRESS Ctrl + Ins (**Copy**).

6 PRESS Shft + Ins (**Paste**).

7 CLICK AND DRAG the new copy between the first and second guides.

8 REPEAT step 6 three times and CLICK AND DRAG each new copy between the guidelines below the last copy.

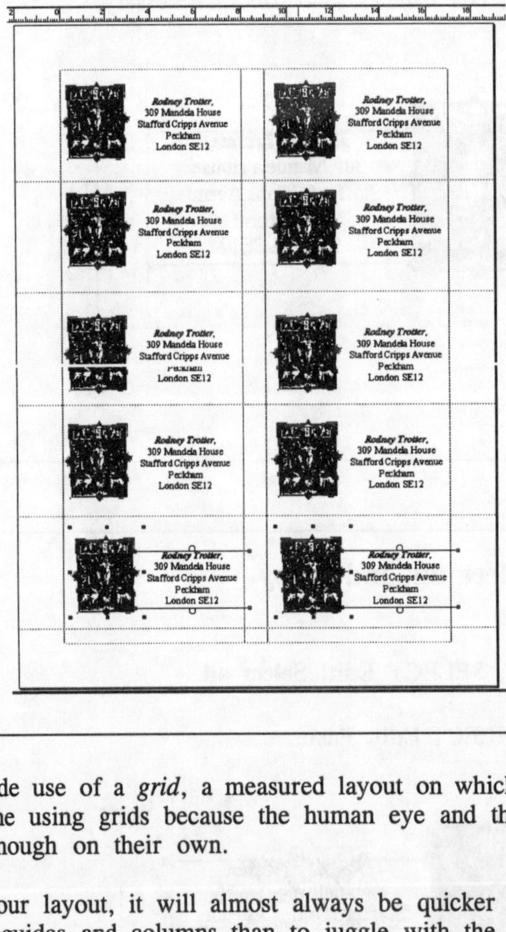

You have now made use of a *grid*, a measured layout on which text and pictures are placed. Most layout is done using grids because the human eye and the computer screen are not usually accurate enough on their own.

However simple your layout, it will almost always be quicker and more accurate to create a grid using rulers, guides and columns than to juggle with the items and guess where they should be placed. This grid was created using columns, because that is a very quick and accurate way of splitting a page into two equal halves.

Apart from making up the rules on a simple grid, guides are also used extensively to position a single item of graphics or text accurately.

Task 13 Creating a customised grid

➢ This task will show you how to set guides and move the ruler zero point

The grid you created in the last activity was as simple as possible, merely a way of creating ten equal areas on a single sheet of A4. Grids can be used many times if they are turned into templates by using the Template option in the Save As... dialogue box. Once a template has been saved, it must be renamed every time it is opened and can be used to repeat the same page layout tens or hundreds of times (as for example in a business newsletter where the same design may be almost identical from one issue to the next, even though the text is almost entirely different).

PageMaker provides several very useful ways of making it easier to place items using guides: **Snap to guides**, **Snap to rulers**, and **Zero lock**. When **Snap to guides** is toggled on, any item moved within a pre-set distance of a guide will jump towards the guide and lock on to it. **Snap to rulers** works in a similar way with two guides that intersect. Any item moved towards the place where the two guides intersect will lock to both, placing the corner of a rectangular item in the right angle created by the intersection.

Toggled off, the **Zero lock** command enables you to move the zero starting point of both horizontal and vertical rulers into any position on the page. This can considerably simplify measuring distances on screen, since unfortunately none of the common paper sizes have a shape that fits neatly into either metric or imperial units. A4, the commonest size for cut paper for example, measures 21 x 29.7 cm or 8.3 x 11.7 in, so even division into four requires considerable fiddling with decimal points. Moving the zero point can make accurate positioning much simpler.

To move the zero point, toggle off the **Zero lock** and click and drag the zero point box located under the Menu control box. Once in the right position, **Zero lock** can be toggled on to prevent it being moved accidentally.

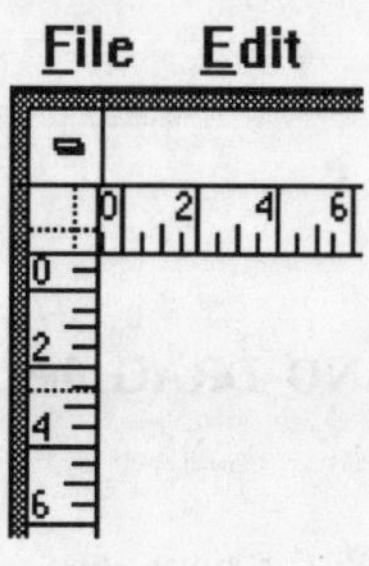

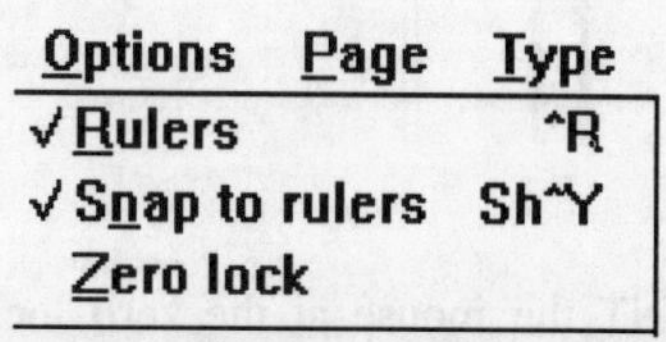

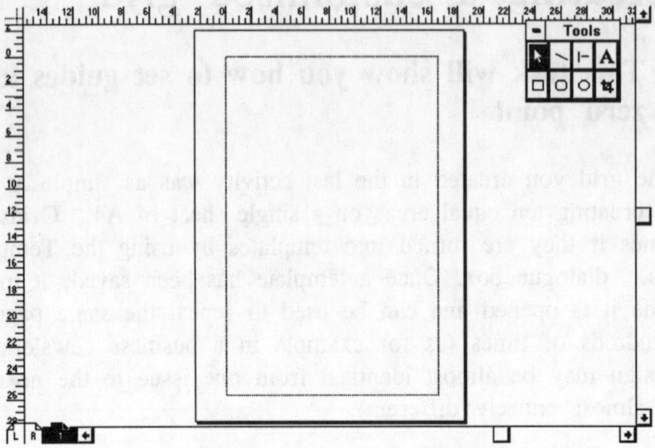

In the picture above, the zero point has been set to the left-hand corner of the margin. Although it is good practice to position guides accurately before placing items, beginners usually find it easier to place items first; so in the activities which follow, guides have been set after items have been placed, to make the process easier to follow.

Activity 13.1 Setting Zero lock

1 Use **File, New** defaults to open new document. TOGGLE off **Options, Zero lock** if it is already set as a default.

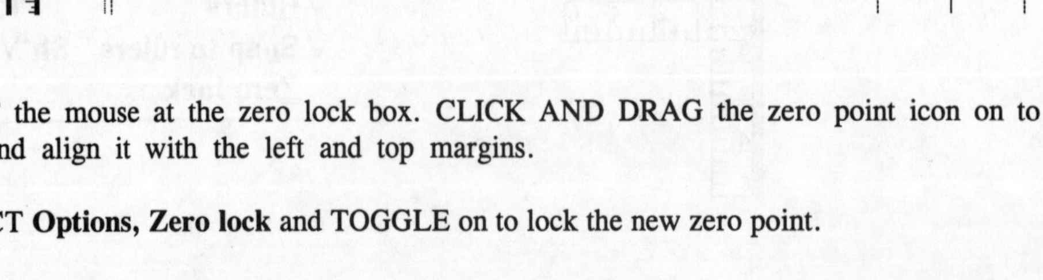

2 POINT the mouse at the zero lock box. CLICK AND DRAG the zero point icon on to the page and align it with the left and top margins.

3 SELECT **Options, Zero lock** and TOGGLE on to lock the new zero point.

Activity 13.2 Setting guides

1 On page 1, set margins to **20** mm.

2 SET **Options, column guides...** to **1**.

3 POINT the mouse at the vertical ruler and CLICK AND DRAG guides to **-10, 10, 130, 160** and **180** mm.

4 SET horizontal guides to **10, 20, 180, 220** mm.

Activity 13.3 Using Place with CLICK AND DRAG

1 In your new document, PLACE **MAST.TIF** near the top of the page.

2 SELECT **Edit, Place** and **FRIEND.TXT**. The screen pointer changes into a text icon.

3 CLICK AND DRAG the text box handles between the **-10** and **180** mm vertical guides.

4 Copy **MAST.TIF** and paste near the bottom of the page.

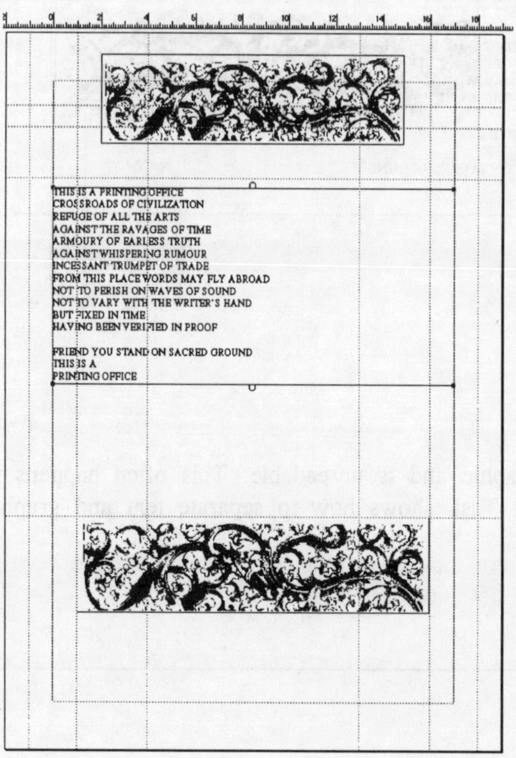

Activity 13.4 Applying Snap to guides and Snap to rulers

1 Still in your new document, SELECT **Options** and TOGGLE on **Snap to guides** and **Snap to rulers**.

2 With the pointer tool selected, CLICK AND DRAG the **FRIEND.TXT** text box so that the left side of it locks to the left-hand guide.

3 CLICK AND DRAG the top **MAST.TIF** graphic so that its top and left sides lock to the horizontal and second vertical guide.

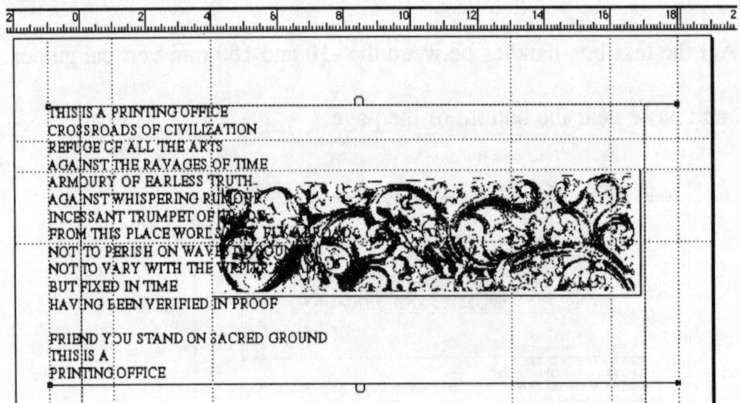

Note that text runs over graphic and is unreadable. This often happens when the **Place** command is used. The next Task shows how to separate text and graphics using the **Text wrap...** command.

Task 14 Laying out pictures and text

➢This task will teach you about sizing and scaling pictures, applying Text wrap and Standoff

You will often need to adjust the size of a picture on your page, and this can be done simply by selecting the pointer tool and clicking and dragging on a convenient handle. You can avoid distorting the *aspect ratio* (the ratio between the height and width) of a picture when resizing, by holding down the Shft key.

When you place pictures and text on a page, you need to determine how much space there will be between them. This is done primarily with the **Text wrap** command and Standoff options. If text runs into a picture accidentally it will be hard to read and look both messy and unprofessional. If text is run over a picture deliberately it needs to be done carefully so that the text is still legible. This can be difficult, and you will almost always have to run off a proof to see whether it works on paper even if it looks perfectly acceptable on screen.

The **Text wrap...** option allows you to choose how text will wrap around pictures.

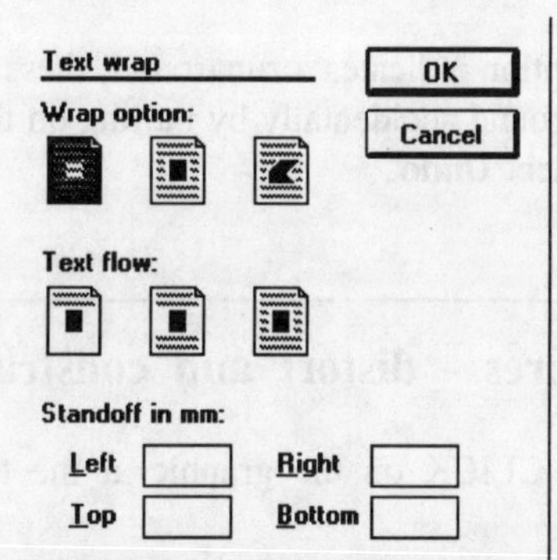

Select one of the the three Wrap option: icons. Do not forget to select an item or graphic first, otherwise your settings will only apply as a default to the next item you place.

Selecting the first icon (usually the default) lets text run over the graphic as it did in Task 13. It is mainly used for putting text on top of plain graphic backgrounds such as tint boxes. 

 Selecting the second Wrap option: icon allows you to choose one of the three Text flow: icons. These give you a choice of having text flow only above a picture,  above and below  or round both sides. 

The third Wrap option, where text flows around an irregularly-shaped graphic, will be selected automatically if you create an irregular standoff. A standoff, which is set in the boxes below the wrap and flow icons, determines the distance

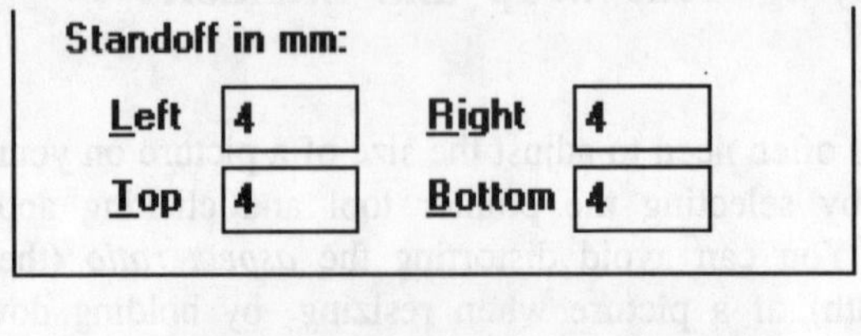

between text and picture. Do not crowd the text and pictures together: the default of 4 mm is a reasonable minimum.

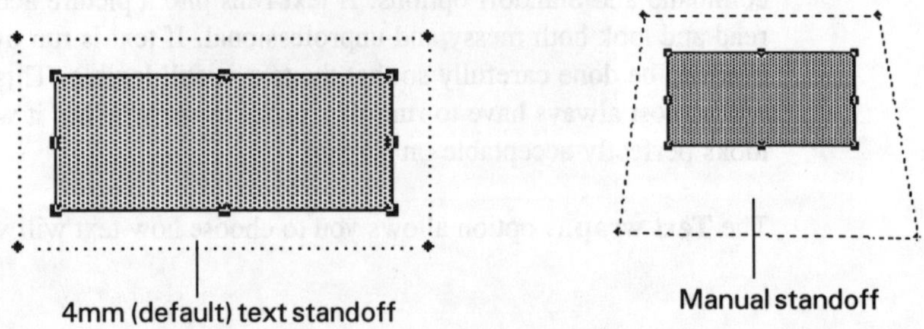

The third Wrap option indicates a runaround; these are described in detail below but if you create a runaround accidentally by pulling on the standoff line rather than a picture handle, simply select **Undo**.

Activity 14.1 **Resizing pictures - distort and constrain**

1 With the pointer tool selected, CLICK on the graphic at the top of the page to select it.

2 POINT the mouse at the lower right-hand handle. CLICK AND DRAG the handle to the 130 mm vertical guide and 40 mm horizontal guide down the third column guide. *Note* the resulting distortion.

3 SELECT the lower graphic. PRESS the Shft key and DRAG the handle in the top-right corner of the graphic to the 160 mm vertical guide.

4 *Note* that the original height and width (*aspect*) ratio are maintained: the picture does not distort.

5 SAVE AS **friend.pm4.**

Activity 14.2 Changing font size

1 SELECT **Options, Text wrap** and TOGGLE on the left-hand Wrap option icon.

2 SELECT the text tool. POINT the mouse anywhere in the text and CLICK to position the cursor in the text.

3 PRESS Ctrl + A to select all text.

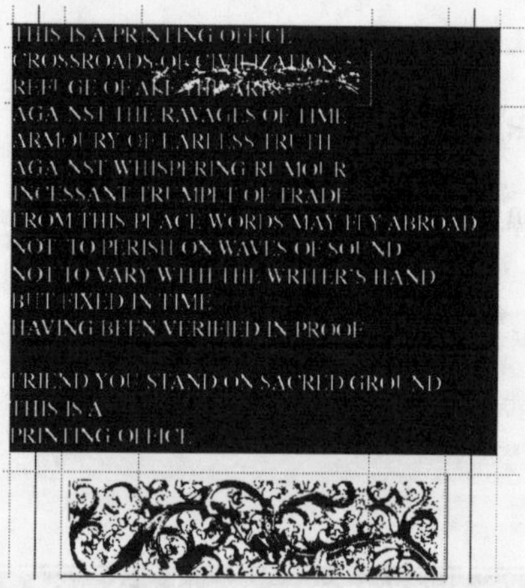

4 SELECT **Type, Size**. SCROLL to 24 points and SELECT.

Activity 14.3 Applying Text wrap

1 SELECT **Options, Text wrap** to display the Text wrap dialogue box.

2 *Note* that, in the default options, the text runs over the graphic.

3 SELECT the middle icon in both the Wrap option: and the Text flow: option. A Standoff default of 4 mm appears.

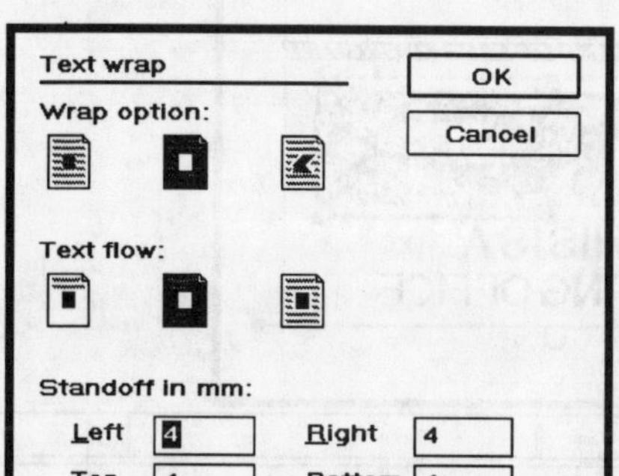

Activity 14.4 Formatting text

1 SELECT the text tool and SELECT all text. PRESS Shft + Ctrl + C. (**Type, Alignment, Align centre**).

2 SELECT **Type**, **Font**, **Times**, and **Style**, **Italic**.

3 POINT the mouse to position the cursor in the first line of text. TREBLE CLICK to select the line.

4 SELECT **Type**, **Style**, **Bold**, and **Size 36** pt. TOGGLE **Italic** off.

5 SELECT the last two lines and FORMAT the font to **GillSans Bold**.

6 DOUBLE CLICK on "WORDS" in line eight and FORMAT as bold .

7 SAVE and PRINT.

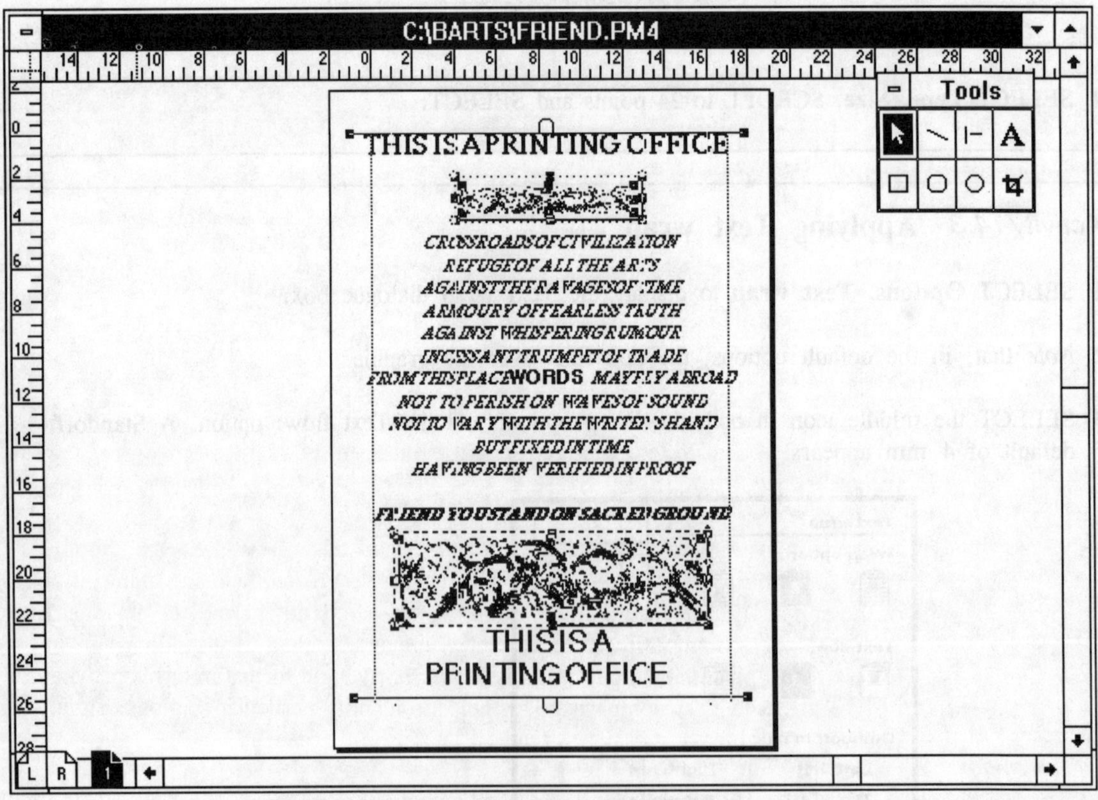

Section D

Creating complex documents

Task 15: Using the Story editor
Task 16: Using Place… and drag
Task 17: Spell checking and using Find…/Change…
Task 18: The Paragraph… command
Task 19: Creating a drop cap
Task 20: Scaling a picture and using the cropping tool
Task 21: Using the Line command
Task 22: Using Fill and Send to back/Bring to front
Task 23: Tabs and leaders
Task 24: The Style palette
Task 25: Applying Autoflow to control text flow
Task 26: Using tracking and leading
Task 27: Creating a runaround
Task 28: Creating bullets
Task 29: Text rotation…, Force justify, Paragraph rules and automatic page numbering

Task 15 Using the story editor

➢ **This task shows you how to use the story editor as a word processor**

The rather daunting list of tasks above are all different ways of formatting text on the page. Formatting text often represents much of the real work that goes into a layout in dtp.

Every publication has its own identity in terms of how it uses typography (different styles of type) on the page. This identity is created by using many, if not all of the options above, almost all of which can be seen in any newsletter, or magazine. Although very common, these formatting commands are not used randomly or in excess. Most professional publications have a fairly rigid format in terms of what kinds of type are used on which pages. This helps to identify particular sections of the publication and make it easier to read.

Beware of using more than a few different typefaces in any one publication, as it will look messy, confused and hard to read. By all means experiment, but in general, good page design is often almost transparent. Only an experienced eye will notice it; the general reader will look straight through it to the contents it carries, unless they get distracted by mistakes or experiments that look unprofessional.

Most text formatting is easily done using the Story editor. This is PM4's own text editor, a sort of built-in word processor, and represents a very significant improvement on earlier versions of PageMaker. It is a good basic text editor which can be opened with a single command: **Edit, Edit story** or Ctrl + E or by clicking three times on the text box with the mouse and the pointer tool (not the text tool) selected.

You can use any of PM4's text formatting commands within the Story editor, although some commands (such as **Type, Font**) will not be displayed on screen until you return to layout view. Due to the limitations of IBM DOS, scrolling through a long story in Story editor can be very slow. This is a good reason for keeping each document file small.

A number of commands, including **Edit, Find.../Change...** or **Spelling...,** can only be activated with the Story editor open. You may find this confusing at first if you are accustomed to an earlier version of the program.

Using the **Close** command or double clicking in the Story editor Menu control box (not the main PageMaker menu) will close this window and return you to layout view with all changes or new text entries entered on the page. This can be much faster than any transfer between PM4 and a word processor.

If the story has not already been placed on the page, closing the Story editor window will produce the following alert:

Click on **Place** to return to layout view with the story loaded into the screen pointer as if you had used the **Edit, Place** command. Simply click on the page where you want the text to start from. Do not use the **Discard** option unless you want to delete everything in your Story editor window, since you will not be able to get it back once it has been discarded.

Story editor is extremely useful for a number of reasons. While it is perfectly normal and acceptable to type small portions of copy (such as picture captions) or small corrections directly on to the page using the text tool, you should avoid doing this for text longer than a couple of sentences, because it is slow. The screen often lags behind the keyboard, it is often hard to read (even with frequent use of the **Page, View** commands) and in some type styles, such as italic, it is almost impossible to see whether word spacing is correct.

Story editor is ideal for corrections and inputting completely new text. Use a word processor if text has been input on a different machine, which may not have PM4 installed, or if you want to do complex formatting which is beyond the power of the Story editor, but make sure before you start any major piece of work that the correct text filter is in place and that PM4 can import your file without significant conflicts, or you may find yourself having to re-edit or reformat the story in PM4.

In this task you are going to open the Story editor, type in some text and format it before placing it on the page as the masthead (title) of a newsletter. You will be using the **Type, Type specs...** command which is a very rapid way of formatting selected text, because it gives you virtually the whole of the **Type menu** in a single dialogue box.

One of the text format options will be new to you: **Type, Set width**. This is used to increase (or decrease) the width of certain characters to give them more impact and is often used on the name of a publication. However, it only works with certain printers, on others it will only increase the spacing between letters.

You will also be using a new font called Wingdings. This is a symbol font used to create non-alphanumeric characters to draw attention to something or make text more lively. Used sensibly these can be fun – do experiment with them but do not try and run them in a large point size; they are designed to be small and, like many free or cheap fonts, at large sizes they develop jagged (bit-mapped) edges.

Activity 15.1 Inputting text into Story editor

1 OPEN a new document, and SCROLL to **A5** in the Page: box. SET all margins to **15** mm apart from Inside: which is set to 20 mm.

2 SET **Options, Column guides...** to **2** with a gutter width of **5** mm.

3 OPEN the first document page (not **Master page**) and SELECT **Edit, Edit story**. A blank Story editor will open.

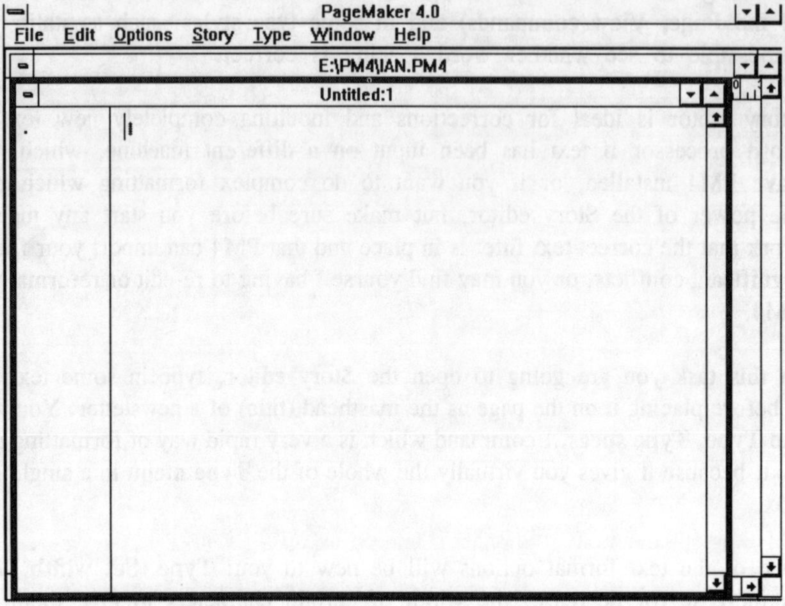

4 TYPE **WALFORD** and then PRESS Enter.

5 On the next line TYPE **GREEN NEWS** and PRESS Enter.

6 On the third line TYPE []][.

Activity 15.2 Using Type specs... to format text

1 SELECT the first line and then **Type, Type specs...**. Depending on your defaults the following box will appear:

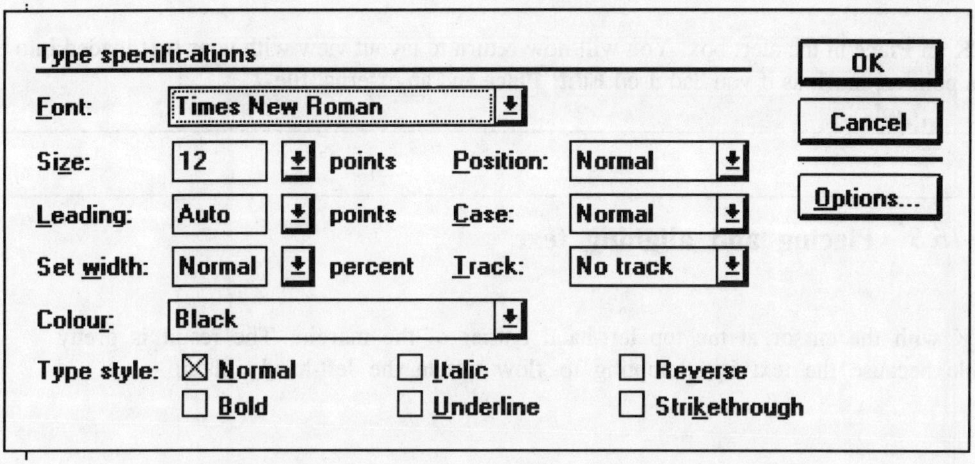

2 SCROLL to **Gill Sans** in the Font: option box and SELECT.

3 SELECT **36** points in the Size: option box and **Bold** in the Type style: option.

4 SCROLL to Set width: **130** per cent.

5 SELECT the second line of text and SET it as **Zapf Chancery**, **36** points. If Zapf Chancery is not available try **Times New Roman**, Type style: **Italic**.

6 SELECT the third line of text and set it as **Wingdings**, **12** points.

7 *Note* that in using Type specifications you cannot set text alignment (centre, justify etc) and that in **Edit story** view, changing the **Font**: makes no apparent difference on screen.

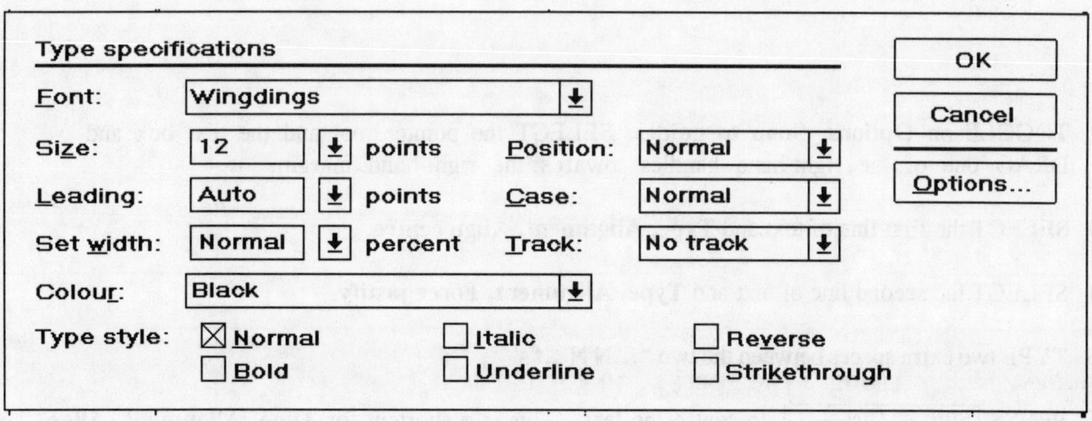

8 DOUBLE CLICK on the Menu control box and an alert will appear.

9 CLICK on **Place** in the alert box. You will now return to layout view with your text loaded into the screen pointer, much as if you had used **Edit, Place** and an external file.

Activity 15.3 Placing and aligning text

1 CLICK with the cursor at the top left-hand corner of the margin. The result is pretty horrible because the text is attempting to flow within the left-hand column.

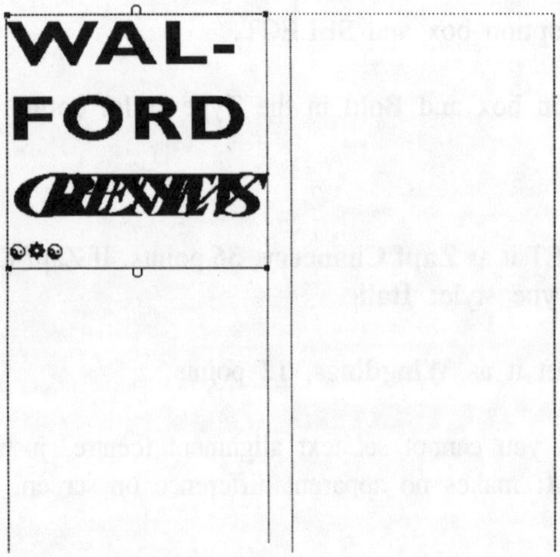

2 TOGGLE on **Options, Snap to guides**. SELECT the pointer tool and the text box and DRAG one of the right-hand handles towards the right-hand margin.

3 SELECT the first line of text and **Type, Alignment, Align centre**.

4 SELECT the second line of text and **Type, Alignment, Force justify**.

5 TYPE two extra spaces between the two "…N N…"s.

6 PRESS Shft + Ctrl + C to centre the text. (This is a shortcut for **Type, Alignment, Align centre**.) Your masthead should now resemble the following illustration:

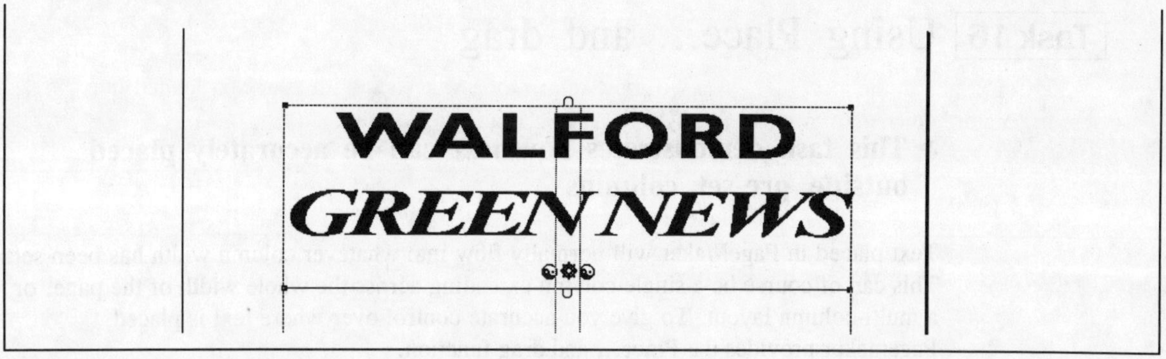

Activity 15.4 **Placing guides and moving columns**

1 Make sure **Options, Zero lock** is toggled off and then CLICK AND DRAG the zero co-ordinates box down to the top left-hand corner of the page margin.

2 SELECT **Options, Zero lock.**

3 DRAG six horizontal rulers down and PLACE them at **13** mm, **34** mm, **37** mm, **51** mm, **137** mm and **146** mm below the zero point.

4 TOGGLE off **Options, Lock guides.**

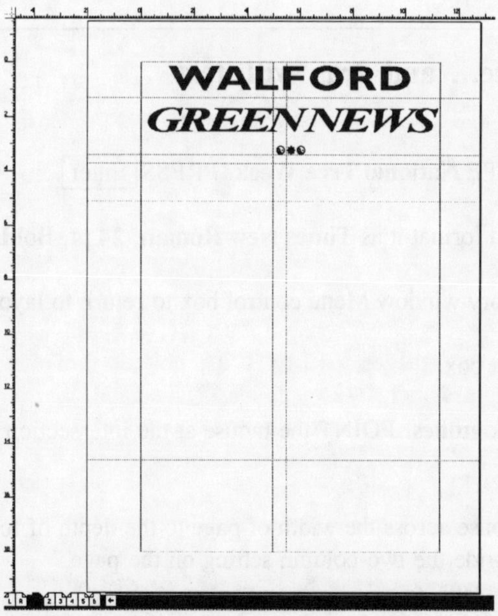

5 CLICK AND DRAG the left-hand column guide to **50** mm.

6 TOGGLE on **Options, Lock guides.**

Task 16 Using Place... and drag

➢This task demonstrates how text can be accurately placed outside pre-set columns

Text placed in PageMaker will normally flow into whatever column width has been set. This can of course be a single column extending across the whole width of the page, or a multi-column layout. To give you accurate control over where text is placed, Pagemaker provides the **Place...** and drag function.

Place... and drag is very simple to use. Select the **Place...** command (either from **Edit, Edit story** or from **File, Place...**), point the mouse at the top left-hand corner of the area over which the text will flow and drag it across and down over the area chosen. A blinking broken-line bounding box will appear as you drag the mouse, and text will be placed across this area once you release the (left-hand) mouse button.

By using horizontal and vertical guides and a 200% page view, text placement can be as precise as using a frame in another dtp program. The same technique can be used for pasting or placing graphics, but this needs care since it will stretch or compress the graphic to fit within the designated area and this kind of distortion only works if it is done deliberately, and sometimes not even then.

Activity 16.1 Using Place... and drag with text

1 OPEN **Edit, Edit story**. TYPE **National Tree Week**. PRESS Enter.

2 SELECT this line of text and format it as **Times New Roman**, **24** pt, **Bold**.

3 DOUBLE CLICK on the Story window Menu control box to return to layout view.

4 CLICK on **Place** in the Alert box.

5 TOGGLE on **Options, Lock guides**. POINT the mouse at the intersection of the third guide and left-hand margin.

6 CLICK AND DRAG the mouse across the width of page to the depth of fourth guide. This allows the **Place** command to over-ride the two-column setting on the page.

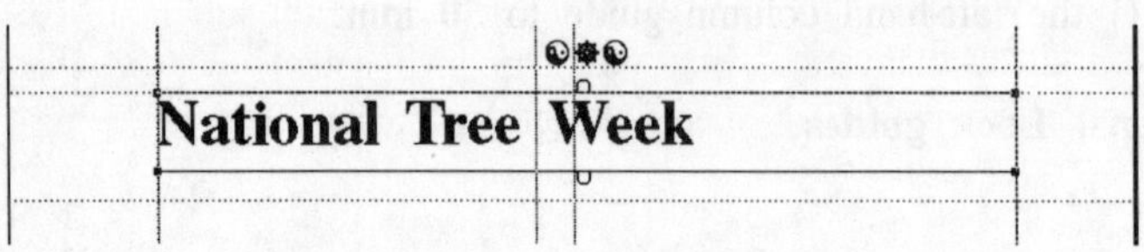

Task 17 Spell checking and using Find.../Change...

➢This is a simple example of how the Spell checker and the Find.../Change... commands work in Story editor

As discussed earlier, PM4 is different from earlier versions in that some text-editing facilities are now available only when the Story editor is open. Two such commands are **Spelling...** and **Find.../Change...**. Both are likely to be familiar if you have done any word processing before. They are quite straightforward, if sometimes rather slow.

Use **Spelling...** every time you create any text, as it will save you time in the long run. We all make both spelling and typing mistakes and this is the fastest way of picking them up. Often shoddy-looking documents are produced in dtp when a few moments taken to check spelling would have removed most if not all the mistakes. Where the spell check will not help you is when you have accidentally mis-typed or mis-spelled a word and produced another word which is in the dictionary. For example in the next task the spell checker ignores "exiting" which is an actual word but a mis-typing of "existing". Remember that the sentence "Spelling chequers are knot infallible" would be passed by a spell check and always allow enough time to proof read properly before producing your final print-out.

When the spell checker finds a word it does not recognise, it gives you a list of possible alternatives and the options Replace, Ignore or Add. Double click on the correct alternative, or type into the Change to: option box and click on Replace. If it highlights a word you have used which it cannot find in its dictionary (like, rather suprisingly, the word "PageMaker") you have a choice between using the Ignore option or clicking on Add, to add the word to PM4's permanent dictionary. If you select Add, another option box appears to give you the choice of Exactly as typed, or Lower case only. The word itself is highlighted and appears in the option box with tildes (~) to indicate where PM4 would normally hyphenate if the word comes at the end of a line. You can remove these if you do not want the word breaks they would produce.

The **Find.../Change...** command is often used to change a frequently used word ('PM4' into 'PageMaker' for example) or to correct formatting changes on imported documents, or to change a dumb quote (`) into a smart quote ('). Consult Appendix C of the PageMaker manual for a list of these special characters entered into the Find.../Change... dialogue box with a carat (^).

The Find.../Change... dialogue box gives you a choice between Find next, Change, Change & find, Change all and Attributes.... Use the Find next and Change & find if there are correct as well as incorrect usages of a character or word. Only use Change all if you are sure that all usages of that item in text are incorrect. By clicking on the Attributes... box you can also select specific font attributes and find and change items in a specific font, type size or type style.

In this exercise you will be checking and placing another two stories on the front page of the newsletter. Type these into the Story editor or your usual word processor from Appendix 1 with the same file names.

You do not have to place a story into layout before opening it in **Edit story**; instead you can open the Story editor and import the file directly and then place it on the page after you have finished working on it.

Activity 17.1 Applying Spelling... to text

1 CLICK on the Pasteboard to deselect any text you may have been working on.

2 OPEN **Edit, Edit story** and then **Story, Import**. (This opens the familiar Place... dialogue box.)

3 FIND **GREEN1.TXT** and DOUBLE CLICK to select it (or type directly into Story editor).

4 SELECT **Edit, Spelling...**

5 When "generaly" appears in the Change to: box, DOUBLE CLICK on "generally" in the alternatives list.

6 When the spell check is complete DOUBLE CLICK on the **Spelling...** window's Menu control box.

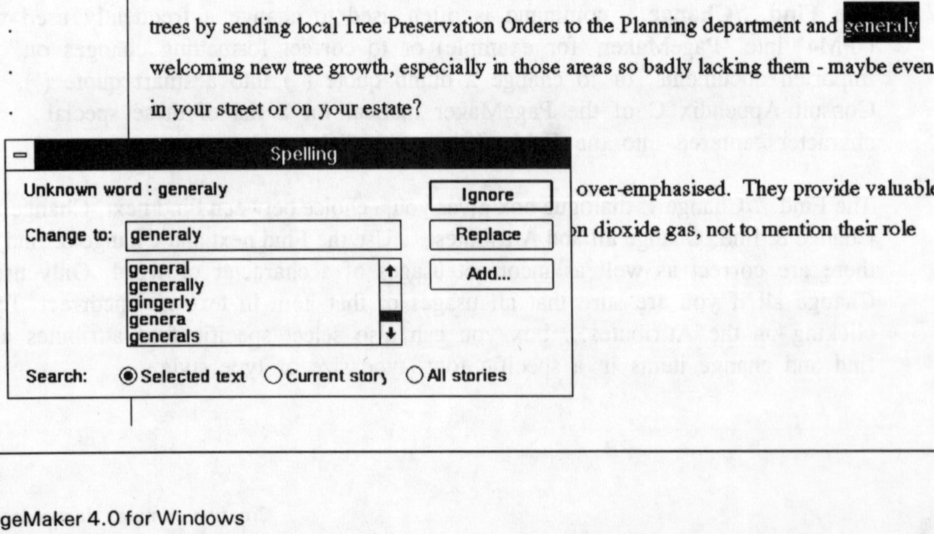

Activity 17.2 Applying Change... to text

1 PRESS [Ctrl + 9]. The Change... box appears.

2 TYPE **exiting** into the Find what: box and **existing** into the Change to: box.

3 CLICK on Find, and then Change.

4 CLICK on the right-hand mouse button to return to Story editor.

Activity 17.3 Changing text to All caps

1 SELECT the first word of the first paragraph and then press [Ctrl + T].

2 SELECT the Case: option and SCROLL to All caps. CLICK on OK. (*This change will not show up until you return to layout view.*)

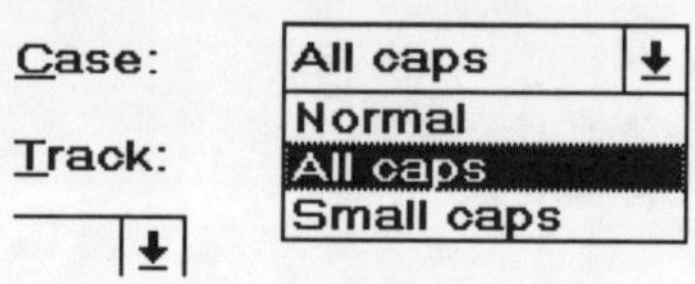

3 SELECT the first paragraph and PRESS [Ctrl + T].

4 SELECT Font: **Times New Roman**, Size: **12** points, (Leading: Auto) and Type style: **Bold**.

5 SELECT the second and third paragraphs and set as the first paragraph but with Size: **10** points.

6 SELECT **Edit, Change**. TYPE a hyphen into the Find what: box and "^ + Shft + -" into the Change to: box.

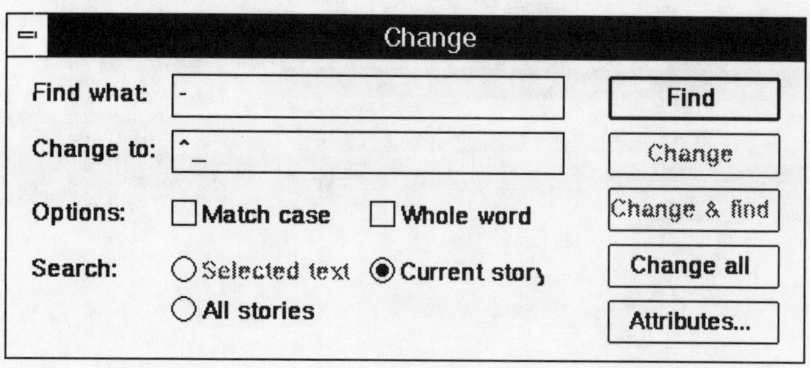

7 SELECT the Find option. When the hyphen in text is located, CLICK on the Change option.

8 CLOSE Story editor and PLACE the text below the fourth horizontal guide.

Activity 17.4 Placing a second piece of text

1 IMPORT (*or type*) **GREEN2.TXT** into Story editor in the same way as **GREEN1.TXT** (*see* activity 17.1).

2 CLICK in the margin next to the first sentence. SELECT it and format as **Bold**, with the first word as **All caps**.

3 PRESS Ctrl + A to highlight all text and then FORMAT it as **GillSans 8** pt with **8** pt leading.

4 SAVE document as **NEWSLETTER**.

Task 18 The Paragraph… command

➢This task shows you how to format paragraphs with indents and line spacing

The **Paragraph…** command can be invoked with **Type, Paragraph…** or Ctrl + M. It enables you to impose a wide range of different paragraph formats on text, the most common of which are the indent first line and alignment settings.

The indent command gives you three choices: indent the whole of the left- or right-hand side of the paragraph and/or indent the first line of the paragraph. Indenting the first line of all paragraphs, except the first, is the commonest format for magazines and books. The alternative, space between paragraphs, which is also available in the Paragraph… option box works well with letters, but can be suprisingly difficult and unwieldy if you try to apply it to a more complex document. (It is also avoided because it takes up additional space on the page.)

The **Paragraph…** command also gives you the chance to set alignment for selected paragraphs either in the Story editor or in layout view. Alignment, unlike most of the text formatting commands, is not available in the Type specs… dialogue box. Once a paragraph format has been set, it forms part of a style which can be imposed on any other piece of text (*see* Style palette page 80).

Do not forget that if you want to apply the **Paragraph…** command to existing text you must select it first. Otherwise it will be applied to text only as you type it in.

Activity 18.1 Justifying text with the Paragraph… command

1 With NEWSLETTER open and the text tool selected, CLICK the screen pointer anywhere in the first story on your page to place the cursor.

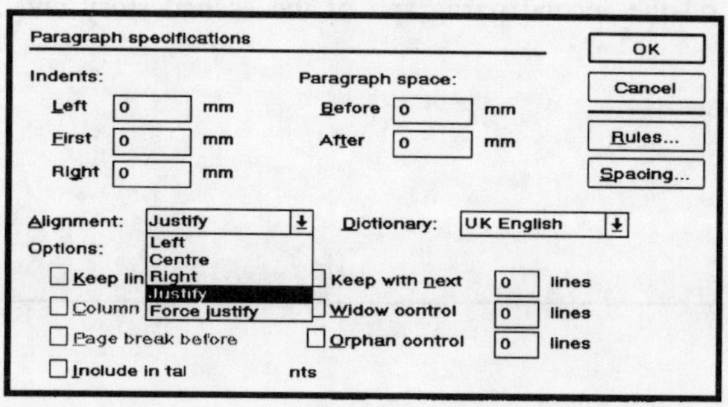

2 SELECT all text in the left-hand column. OPEN **Type, Paragraph...**.

3 POINT to **Alignment**: and SCROLL to select Justify.

4 REPEAT steps 1 to 3 with the second story in the right-hand column.

Activity 18.2 Indenting first lines

1 SELECT the second and third paragraphs of the first story and PRESS Ctrl + M.

2 POINT to the Indents: First option box and DOUBLE CLICK to select contents.

3 TYPE **5** mm and CLICK on OK.

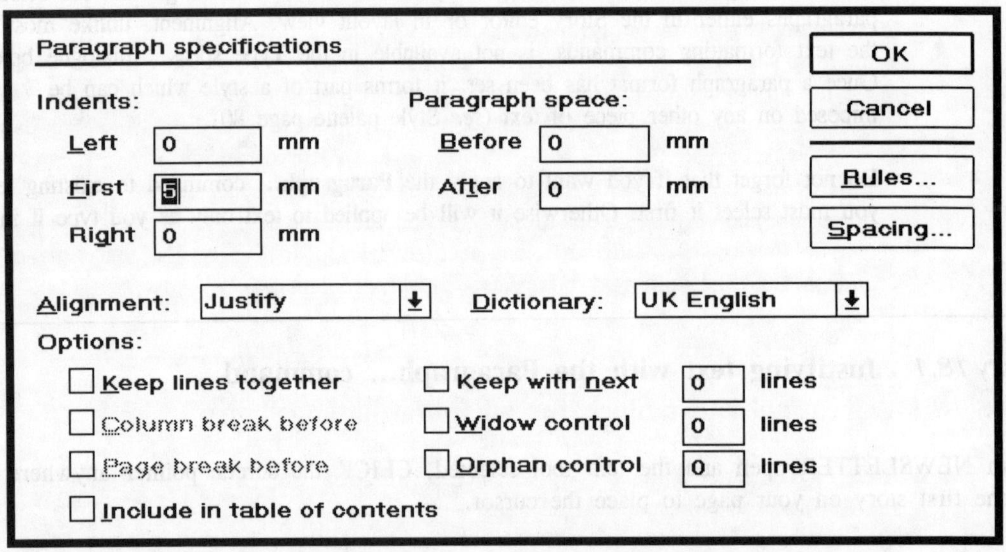

4 REPEAT steps 1 to 3 on the second paragraph of the second story and SAVE.

Task 19 Creating a drop cap

➢This task shows you how to create a drop cap, an ornamental letter to start a story

The main aim of a good layout should be to lead the reader's eye into the story. A common way of doing this in newspaper and magazine layout is the 'drop cap', which means beginning a story with a large capital letter (referred to by Aldus as "enlarged initial letter").

If you have access to a paint program which manipulates text, the easiest way to create a drop cap is to import a single character from the paint program as a graphic using the tiff format. This can then be scaled on the page with text wrap exactly as you would any other graphic.

If a paint program is not available there is also a way of creating a drop cap inside PageMaker. The main point is to convert the initial letter into a separate text block, position it at the begining of the paragraph and then create two text boxes for the remaining text in the paragraph so that the text can be positioned to the right and below the drop cap. This means moving the left-hand handle of the text box to the right, closing up the text box to the required number of lines and then picking up the remainder of the text and positioning it normally in the column below the drop cap.

This is harder to describe than to do, but do not omit the step of including horizontal and vertical guides to the right and below the drop cap, as very few people can do this by eye with sufficient accuracy. Keep an eye on the text flow around a drop cap, the split text boxes can causes problems.

Activity 19.1 Creating a text block for an initial letter

1 With **NEWSLETTER** open and the text tool selected, SELECT the letter "A" which begins the story in the left-hand column and PRESS [Shft + Del] to **Cut** it out of text.

2 POINT the screen pointer onto the Pasteboard and CLICK to place the cursor. PRESS [Shft + Ins] to **Paste** the character.

3 SELECT "A" and PRESS [Ctrl + T].

4 SET to Font: **GillSans**, Size: **32** pt, Type style: **Bold**.

5 DRAG a vertical guide to **64** mm.

6 SELECT the pointer tool and the text of the second story.

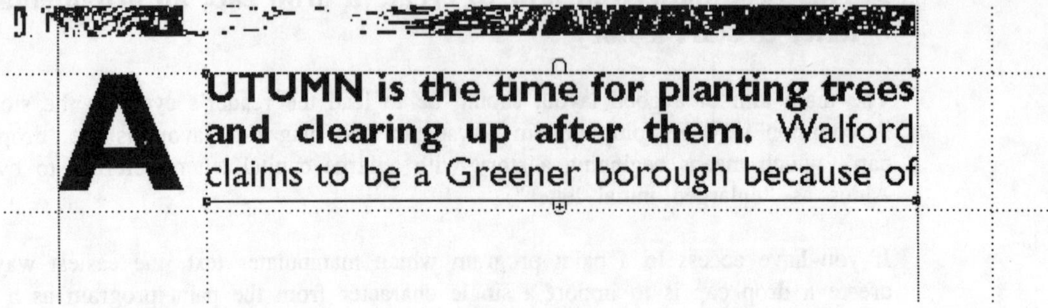
AUTUMN is the time for planting trees and clearing up after them. Walford claims to be a Greener borough because of

7 DRAG the top left-hand handle of the text box to the 64 mm vertical guide and lower the window blind to the 146 mm horizontal guide.

8 SELECT the "A" character text box and align the top of the character to the guide and the left edge with the left-hand column guide.

9 With **Snap to rulers** on, CLICK on the central lower handle of the lower text box to pick up over-matter. CLICK below the intersection of the column guide and the 146 mm horizontal guide to place remaining text.

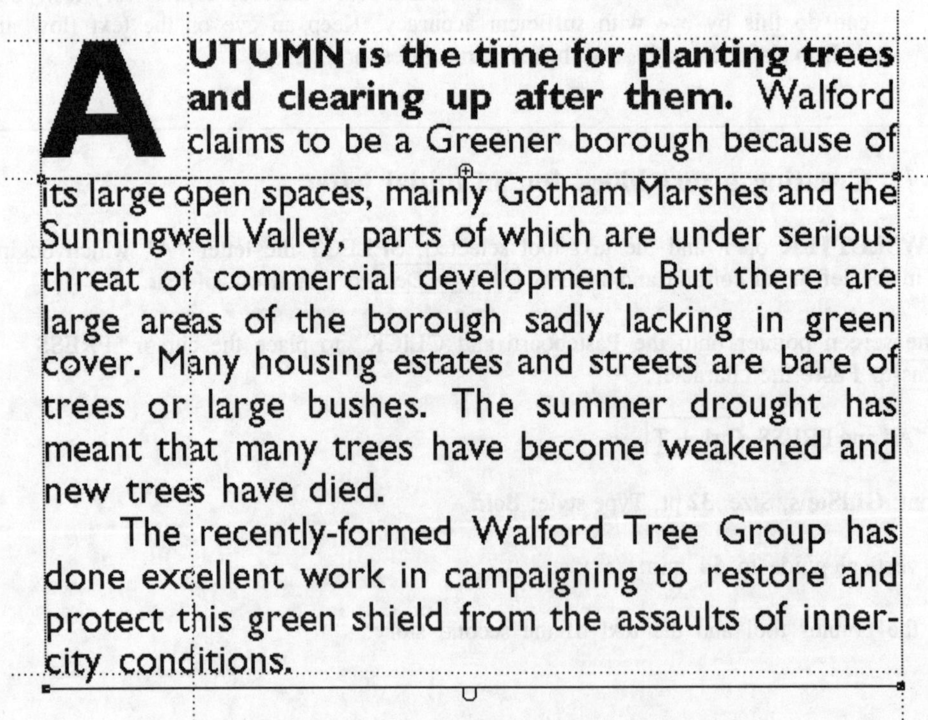
AUTUMN is the time for planting trees and clearing up after them. Walford claims to be a Greener borough because of its large open spaces, mainly Gotham Marshes and the Sunningwell Valley, parts of which are under serious threat of commercial development. But there are large areas of the borough sadly lacking in green cover. Many housing estates and streets are bare of trees or large bushes. The summer drought has meant that many trees have become weakened and new trees have died.

The recently-formed Walford Tree Group has done excellent work in campaigning to restore and protect this green shield from the assaults of inner-city conditions.

Task 20 Scaling a picture and using the cropping tool

➢This task shows how to resize and trim a picture on the page without changing the original

As discussed earlier, PageMaker's approach to layout is to let the user do much of their formatting and arrangement *after* material has been imported on to the page. This is particularly true of pictures or graphics, which are imported on to the page at the same size as they were created.

Usually these pictures need to be resized, or scaled, trimmed or cropped to fit into the rest of the layout. Scaling and cropping a picture in PageMaker is very simple, giving it a significant advantage over conventional layout where pictures are scaled and cropped separately and then dropped into a designated area by the printer. Being able to see a picture in the layout, as you design the page, gives a much better idea of how the final page will look and gives lots of flexibility for trying out different layouts where the effect of the size of the picture can be judged and changed very quickly and at no extra cost other than the time it takes to get a satisfactory result.

There are three ways of changing the shape and size of a graphic: ***scaling***, ***cropping*** and a combination of the two. Graphics can also be modified by the contrast control facility providing you understand the capability of your printer.

Reducing or enlarging (*scaling*) is done by constraining the picture, much as you can constrain an ellipse into a circle (*see* page 14). Simply select the picture, hold down the [Shft] key and drag on the most convenient handle to increase or reduce the size without losing the original proportions (*aspect ratio*) of the image. If you do not hold down the [Shft] key the picture will distort in the direction you drag it. If you make a mistake and distort the picture accidentally, select **Edit, Undo** ([Alt + Bkspce]).

To trim (*crop*) a picture to fit the available space in a layout, select the cropping tool in the bottom-right hand corner of the **Toolbox**. Click on your picture or graphic to select it and then place the cropping tool over a convenient handle (be careful to avoid the standoff handles) and drag in the direction you wish to trim. Repeat with other handles as necessary. Again you can use **Undo** if you make a mistake or select a handle and reverse the trim. Using the cropping tool will not affect your original picture file in any way, and if you want to place the same picture again it will come back in the original size.

You can also use the cropping tool to move the part of the picture which is displayed (and printed) within a cropped area within its new borders. Simply click and drag on the picture itself and the cropping tool will turn into a grabber hand. This will move the image without changing the size, shape, or position of the picture on the page.

Activity 20.1 Placing and constraining a picture

1 With the pointer tool selected, PRESS Ctrl + D to open the **Place** window.

2 SCROLL to select **COMMON1.TIF.**

3 DRAG a vertical guide to **52** mm and CLICK on the intersection between the fourth horizontal guide and the right-hand column guide.

4 SELECT the picture, PRESS Shft and DRAG the top right-hand handle diagonally to the right-hand edge of the page.

5 DRAG the picture up the page until the top of picture aligns with the third horizontal guide.

Activity 20.2 Cropping a picture

1 With the picture selected, SELECT the cropping tool.

2 POINT to the bottom right-hand corner and DRAG towards the right-hand margin.

3 CLICK in the picture and DRAG towards the left in order to centre the image in the frame.

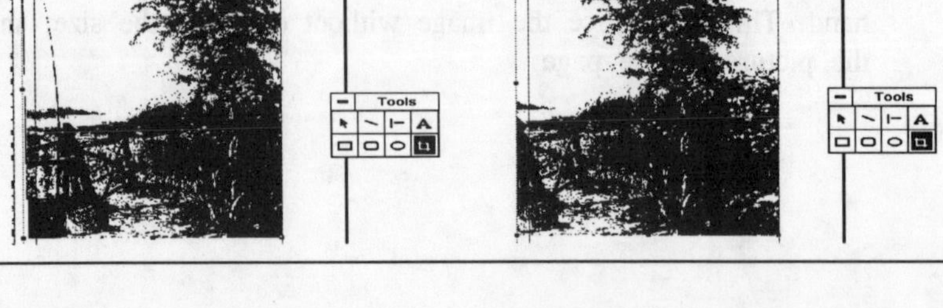

Task 21 Using the Line command

➢This task shows you how to use the line tool

Although PageMaker is not a paint or drawing program, it is capable of a wide range of simple graphic effects. These are used to draw attention to particular items on the page or to make it look more interesting.

Earlier in this guide you used the graphic tools provided by the **Toolbox**, but by using the **Element, Line** or **Element, Fill** commands you can add more sophisticated graphic effects (*see* next task).

Use the **Line** command to choose the width or type of line you want to use with any of the graphic tools. One thing to remember is that this command can only be applied before you use a graphic tool or after you have selected an item. Do not expect PageMaker to read your mind; as with every other command it cannot be applied to any work you have already done unless you select that item first.

One feature, **Reverse line**, needs a little care unless you have a colour monitor. **Reverse line** will produce a white (non-printing) line set according to whichever line style has been toggled on previously. When it is selected you can see its handles, but if it is on a white background and is not selected it will be invisible. Clicking the mouse in an attempt to find an invisible reverse line can be very frustrating so do not reverse a line until it is placed on some kind of background. The quickest way of finding it, if you do make this mistake, is usually to apply **Edit, Select all** (Ctrl + A) with the pointer tool selected. This will show up all items on the page and the reverse line will be in an apparently empty windowblind. (The same trick should be used if you lose reversed text.)

In this exercise you will also be placing a rule under "Walford". (This can be done with **Type, Type style, Underline** but with the font used here the underline is very thin and looks weak.)

Activity 21.1 Drawing a box with a frame

1 PLACE a new file, **CONTENTS.TXT,** below the text in the left-hand column of your document.

2 SELECT **Element, Line** and the three line rule and then the box tool (in the bottom left-hand corner of the Toolbox).

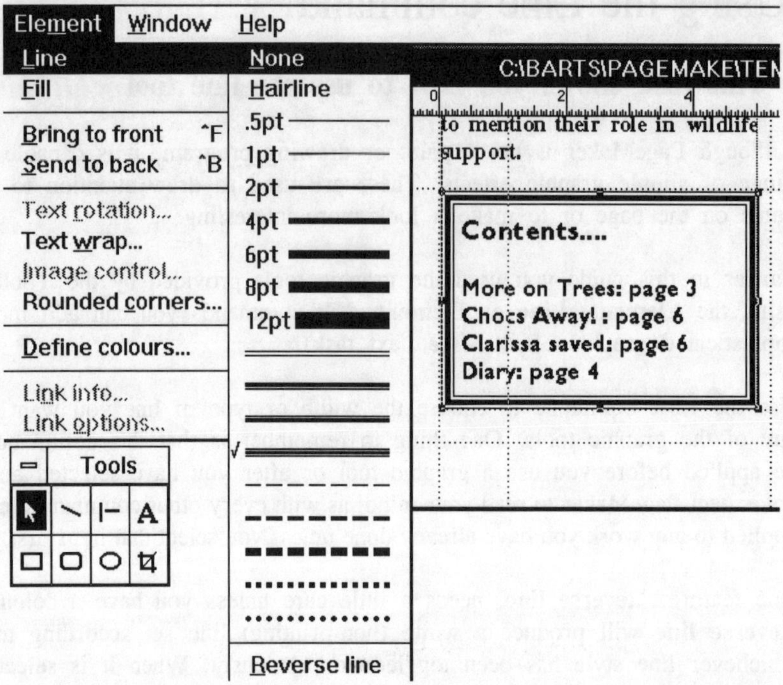

3 POINT the mouse at the intersection of the guide and the left-hand margin below text in the left-hand column.

4 CLICK AND DRAG to the left-hand centre column guide.

5 SELECT the pointer tool to resize or reposition so that the text is aligned with the box.

Activity 21.2 **Drawing a rule**

1 DRAG vertical guides to **11** mm and **102** mm and a horizontal guide to **12** mm.

2 SELECT **Element, Line, 4** pt rule and then the horizontal/vertical line tool.

3 With **Snap to rulers** on, CLICK on the 11 mm vertical and 12 mm horizontal guides and DRAG the rule to the 102 mm vertical guide.

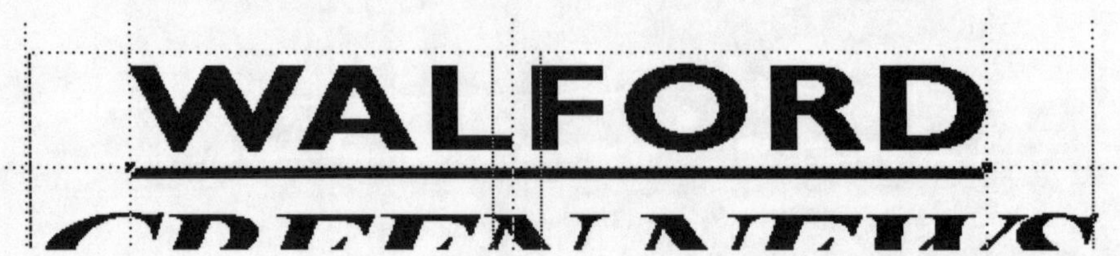

Task 22 Using Fill and Send to back/Bring to front

➢This task shows you how to use the Fill command and how to treat tints as a layer of the page

In order to fill a shape with a tint, you can either select the **Fill** command before using the box tool, rounded-corner box tool or ellipse tool, or you can select a box or ellipse and apply **Fill** after you have drawn it.

Fill gives you a choice of tints from **None** which is transparent, **Paper** which prints white but will hide any text behind it, through 10% gradations to **Solid** which prints as black. (If you have a colour printer **Solid** can be 100% of any colour you apply.) There are also a range of patterns available.

Layouts often use items placed on top or overlapping each other. The printer will only print what is on top and will ignore anything which is hidden underneath the topmost item.

This can be a problem if a larger item has been created after a smaller item, because it will sit on top of the item underneath and hide it. This is a common difficulty with text in a tint box.

You can select any item in a layer by holding down Ctrl and clicking. This will select each item in turn, starting at the top. When the item you want has been selected, select **Element, Bring to front**. If there are only two items, you can select the one on top and use **Element, Send to back.**

Activity 22.1 Using the Fill and Send to Back commands

1 With **NEWSLETTER** open, SELECT the box in the left-hand column and **Element, Fill, 20%**. (*The text is now obscured.*)

2 With the box still selected, SELECT **Element, Send to back** and the text will reappear (and print out) on top of the tint box.

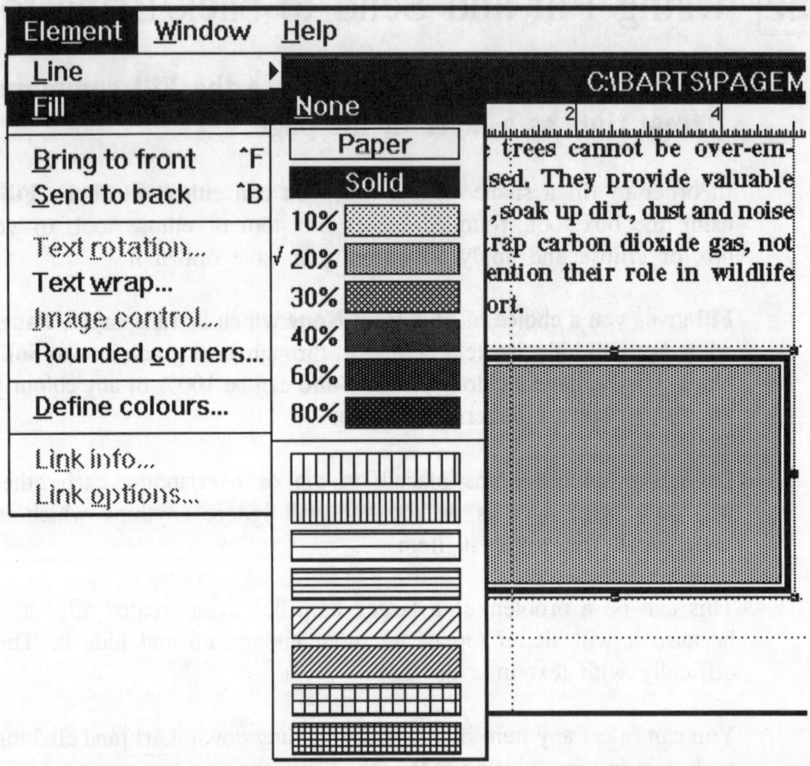

Activity 22.2 **Reversing text**

1 SELECT the text tool and all the Contents text.

2 SELECT **Type, Type style, Reverse.**

Task 23 Tabs and leaders

➢This task demonstrates the use of the Indents/tabs window to place tabs and leaders

If you have set tabs in your word processing program they can be imported into PageMaker directly, though it is often easier to set tabs in layout where you can see how they will work on the page.

Tab setting in PageMaker is done with the **Type, Indents/tabs...** command, which displays tabs and indents with a ruler and an icon display which will also give you a visual representation of any indents you have set in the Paragraph... dialogue box.

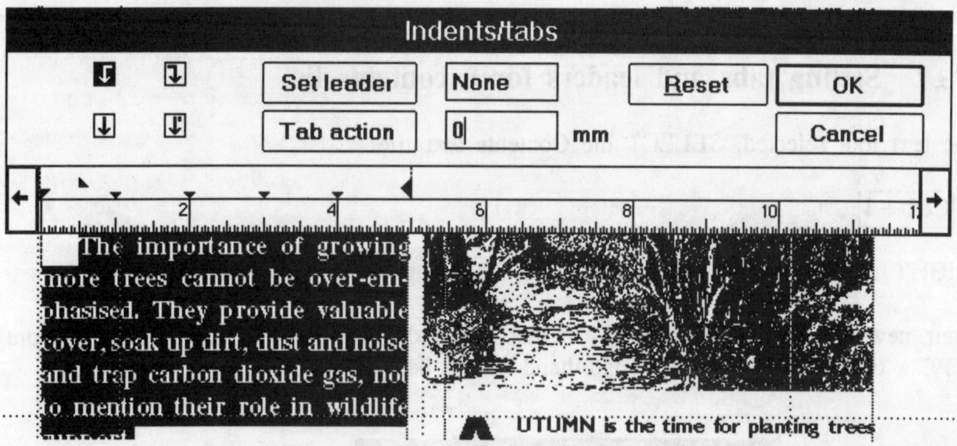

Note that on the far left of the tab ruler the lower triangle indicates the (0) indent of the body text and the second, upper triangle indicates the indent for the first line. Moving one will normally move the other the same distance. Hold down Shft to move the paragraph indent without moving the first line indent.

PageMaker's normal default on tabs is to set one every 10 mm. If you use a particular tab setting frequently, you can set it as a default by creating it when no document is open on the page.

The four tab actions available are left-align, right-align, centre and decimal. Decimal will centre any decimal point at the tab position — indispensable for columns of figures. To create a new tab simply click on the tab type you want and either type the position into the dialogue box or click on the ruler at the point where you want to position the new tab. This will automatically delete any of the default tabs to the left of it. In fact this may be the only way to delete a tab: the Tab action, Delete command will merely replace your tab with a default tab.

The Tab action box will also give you a choice of Add, Move or Repeat a tab at whatever distance you type into the measurement box. The Reset option will cancel all of your tabs and return you to the default positions.

The Set leader box enables you to set dots, dashes, long dashes or any character of your choice (*custom*) in the space between your text and any tab position you highlight on the ruler. This is often used for indexed page numbers in a contents list and you will use it for this in the following activity.

Select the text tool if you want to set tabs in a paragraph where your cursor is located or to apply tabs to selected text. Use the pointer tool to set default tabs for the whole document.

Activity 23.1 Setting tabs and leaders for a contents list

1 With the text tool selected, SELECT the Contents text file.

2 PRESS [Ctrl + I].

3 HIGHLIGHT the left-align tab icon and TYPE **30** mm in the box to place the tab.

4 With your new tab highlighted, CLICK on the Set leader option box, SCROLL to Custom and TYPE a tilde (~) into the top right-hand option box where the (None) default is

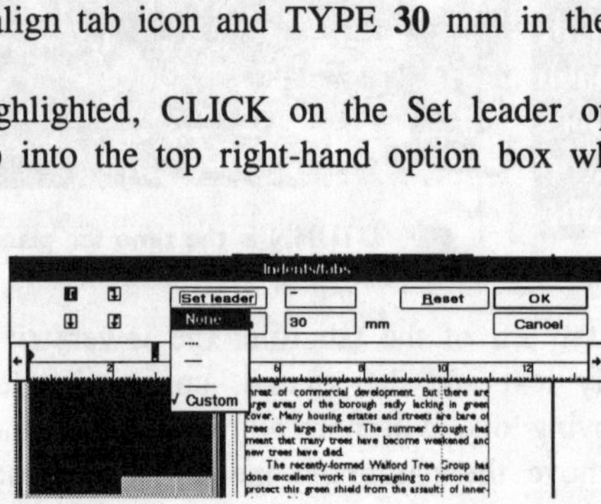

highlighted. CLICK on OK.

5 PLACE the cursor after the colon (:) in the second line of text. PRESS [Tab].

6 REPEAT in the third, fourth and fifth lines of text.

7 DRAG vertical guides to left and right margins.

8 PLACE AND DRAG **ADDRESS.TXT** below bottom margin and between margin guides.

9 FORMAT text as **Gillsans**, **6** pt, **Bold**.

10 SAVE file as **GN1** and print. Your result could look like the following example:

WALFORD
GREEN NEWS

National Tree Week

THE annual Tree Week starts at the end of November when a national focus on tree renewal is organised.

We hope to participate in this and urge local people to adopt a local tree, protect existing trees by sending local Tree Preservation Orders to the Planning department and generally welcoming new tree growth, especially in those areas so badly lacking them — maybe even in your street or on your estate?

The importance of growing more trees cannot be over-emphasised. They provide valuable cover, soak up dirt, dust and noise and trap carbon dioxide gas, not to mention their role in wildlife support.

AUTUMN is the time for planting trees and clearing up after them. Walford claims to be a Greener borough because of its large open spaces, mainly Gotham Marshes and the Sunningwell Valley, parts of which are under serious threat of commercial development. But there are large areas of the borough sadly lacking in green cover. Many housing estates and streets are bare of trees or large bushes. The summer drought has meant that many trees have become weakened and new trees have died.

The recently-formed Walford Tree Group has done excellent work in campaigning to restore and protect this green shield from the assaults of inner-city conditions.

Contents....

AUTUMN 1993 No. 18 Free to Residents of Walford. Published by Walford Green Action Group 071 - 999 9999

Task 24 The Style palette

➢ This task will show you how to use the Style palette to format text

If you are producing a set of similar documents in PageMaker, there is a quick and simple way of formatting any paragraph of text, headlines, or captions without having to set them manually every time you input text.

This is done with the **Style palette**: a list of different type styles which can be displayed permanently on your screen if you toggle on **Window, Style palette**. If you are short of space on your screen you can toggle off **Window, Style palette** but still display your list of styles when you need it as a pulldown menu under **Type, Style**.

Remember that a style can only apply to whole paragraphs; use the **Type** menu to format words, characters or phrases. To apply a style to text, first select all paragraphs you want it to apply to, or place the cursor in the specific, single paragraph you want to format and then scroll to the name of the style in the **Style Palette** or **Type, Style** command. If you are in Story editor you can toggle on **Options, Display style names** to have the style name of each paragraph displayed in the adjacent margin. (*The Story editor itself will only show a few aspects of style, such as Bold or Italic.*)

The Style palette gives you a series of default styles, but you can create your own by using the **Type, Define styles...** command and the New option. The Based on: option will give the properties of any existing style. Selecting New will give you access to the **Type specs...**, **Paragraph...** and other dialogue boxes. You can also Edit an existing style by selecting it and typing in new values. The Copy option allows you to retrieve an existing style from another document by selecting the *.PM4 document which contains the style(s) you want.

Generally people find it easiest to work out a suitable format on the page and then, when they are happy with how it looks, use it to create a new style. This is very simply done by selecting part of the text and **Type, Define styles...** and then, with Selection highlighted, clicking on New and typing in a name for the new style.

This saves all the bother of defining each aspect of the format under New. If you have already created a text format for a paragraph using the **Type menu** commands this will be listed as No style. Create and name a new style based on No style if you are likely to want to use it again.

Any style you create will be specific to the document it is created in, and you cannot create styles that apply automatically to all subsequent documents. There are three ways around this. The first is to use the **Define styles...**, Copy option, the second is by using a template created under **Save as...**, Template from an existing document, and the third is to **Copy** and **Paste** text from one document to another. The pasted text will import its style automatically into the **Style palette** in the new document.

The activities below will create two new styles which can be applied to subsequent text in the newsletter. To ensure that any changes you make do not affect your original file you will begin by opening a copy of the original file which you can save with another name, leaving the original file intact.

Activity 24.1 Opening Style palette and applying default styles

1 SELECT **File**, OPEN **NEWSLET1** and CLICK on Copy.

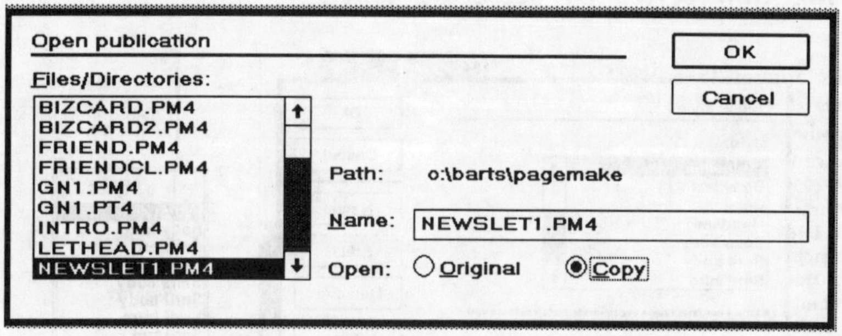

2 With the text tool selected, POINT at the left-hand column, CLICK to place the cursor anywhere in the body text and TREBLE CLICK to select the paragraph.

3 SELECT **Window**, and TOGGLE on **Style Palette**.

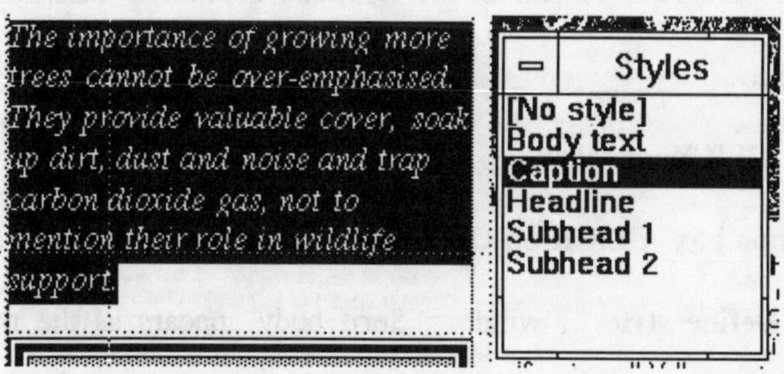

4 CLICK on Headline to select it in the **Style palette** and *note* the change in type style.

5 POINT to the second paragraph of text in the left-hand column and CLICK to place the cursor.

6 TOGGLE on Body text style and note the change in type style.

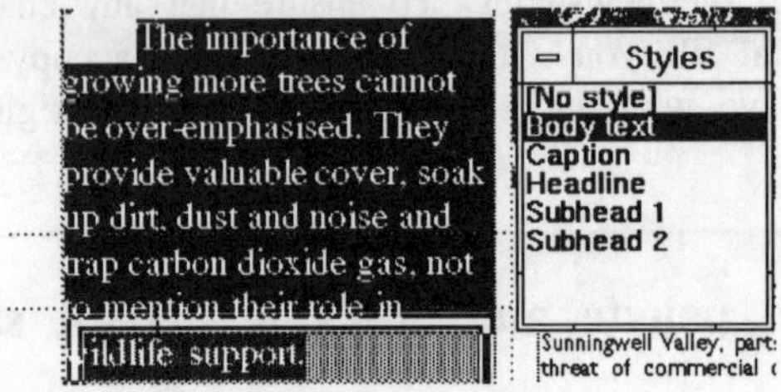

Activity 24.2 Creating new styles by selecting text

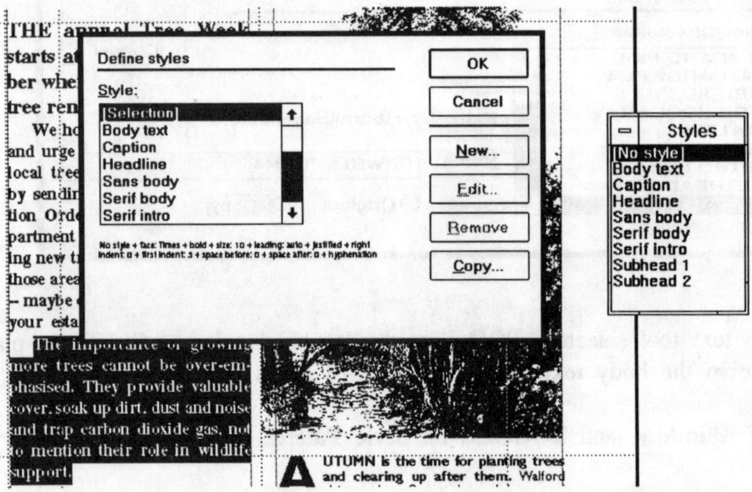

1 TREBLE CLICK in the third paragraph of text in the left-hand column to SELECT.

2 SELECT **Type, Define styles…**.

3 With [Selection] highlighted, CLICK on New….

4 TYPE **Serif body** into the option box. CLICK on OK. (*New… dialogue box closes*.)

5 CLICK on OK to close the **Define styles…** window. Serif body appears as the new option in the **Styles** window.

6 REPEAT steps 1 to 5 with the first paragraph of the story and name the new style **Serif intro**.

7 REPEAT steps 1 to 5 with the second paragraph of text in the right-hand column and name the new style **Sans body**.

8 SAVE the document as **STYLE1**.

Task 25 Applying Autoflow to control text flow

➢ This task will show you how to flow text automatically into new columns and pages

If you have tried experimenting with your own layouts, you may already have encountered problems with text flow. Almost everybody does when they first learn PageMaker. Text flow in PageMaker is fairly simple, but you need to be clear about the basic rules.

When you **Place...** text, PageMaker gives you a choice about how the text will flow on to the page. Text will normally flow down whatever column you **Place...** it in, until it reaches the bottom of the page or the end of the text. But if your text is longer than a single column, you should toggle on **Options, Autoflow** before you **Place...** the text. Text will then flow into any other columns on the page. If you have toggled on Autoflow with the **Master pages** open first, and then go to the page where you are placing text, new pages will be created automatically if there is more text than room on the page where you place the text. (In other words, you cannot create new pages automatically if Autoflow is only active on your page and not the whole document.)

If **Autoflow** is toggled off, a long piece of text will flow to the end of the column, which may cover the whole page, and then stop. The remainder of the text (called overmatter) will be hidden inside a triangle in the central handle on the bottom edge of the text box (a # symbol in previous versions of PageMaker).

You can place this hidden, additional, text by clicking on that triangle. (Use a larger page view if you have trouble locating it with your screen pointer.) This will load up your screen pointer with the overmatter and when you click elsewhere, this text will flow into a new text box linked to the first. The text is "threaded" together, as Aldus puts it, and this means for example, that if you delete a line from the first text box, the text in the next box will move up.

Do not use **Copy** and **Paste** for overmatter. This is a very common mistake which often creates a lot of unnecessary work in rethreading the pasted text back into text flow. Once text has been copied and pasted, it has no link with previous text. This is useful, however, for headlines, quotes and captions which have been written as part of a story, but which need to be separated from the main text.

In general, leave **Autoflow** toggled on unless you want to put overmatter onto the pasteboard. Click on the (red) triangle in the bottom window blind and then click on the pasteboard to run out the overmatter. You can then cut and rewrite the text and see how much is still left over. To see the pasteboard use Ctrl + Shft + W or Ctrl + Shft + 0.

You can always see by the shape of the screen pointer whether **Autoflow** is on or off. If it is on, the screen pointer will be in the shape of a double arrow; if it is off, it will be an icon that resembles a piece of text. (*See* page 42.)

If you have loaded your screen pointer with text using the **Place...** command, and it is in the wrong mode, simply select **Options, Autoflow** and you can toggle it on or off, without losing your text. You can also move to another page by clicking on the page icon, again without losing any text held by the screen pointer.

In the first activity below, you will be placing the same text with **Autoflow** off and then deleting it and placing it again with **Autoflow** on, in order to see the difference.

Activity 25.1 Inserting pages and using Place... with Autoflow off

1 With **NEWSLET1** open, SELECT **Page, Insert pages...**.

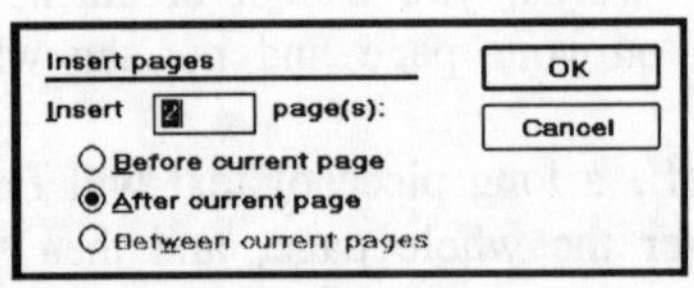

2 CLICK on OK for the default of 2 page(s), After current page. The document will open on the second page.

3 SELECT **Options, Column guides** and set to **2** with 5 mm (default) Space between columns.

4 SELECT **Options, Autoflow** and TOGGLE off.

5 With the pointer tool selected, PLACE **GREEN3.TXT** file in the top left-hand corner of the left-hand column. *Note* that the text runs to the bottom of the column and stops there.

6 CLICK on the triangle in the handle of the lower window blind and *note* the change in the screen pointer.

7 CLICK in the top left-hand corner of the second (right-hand) column.

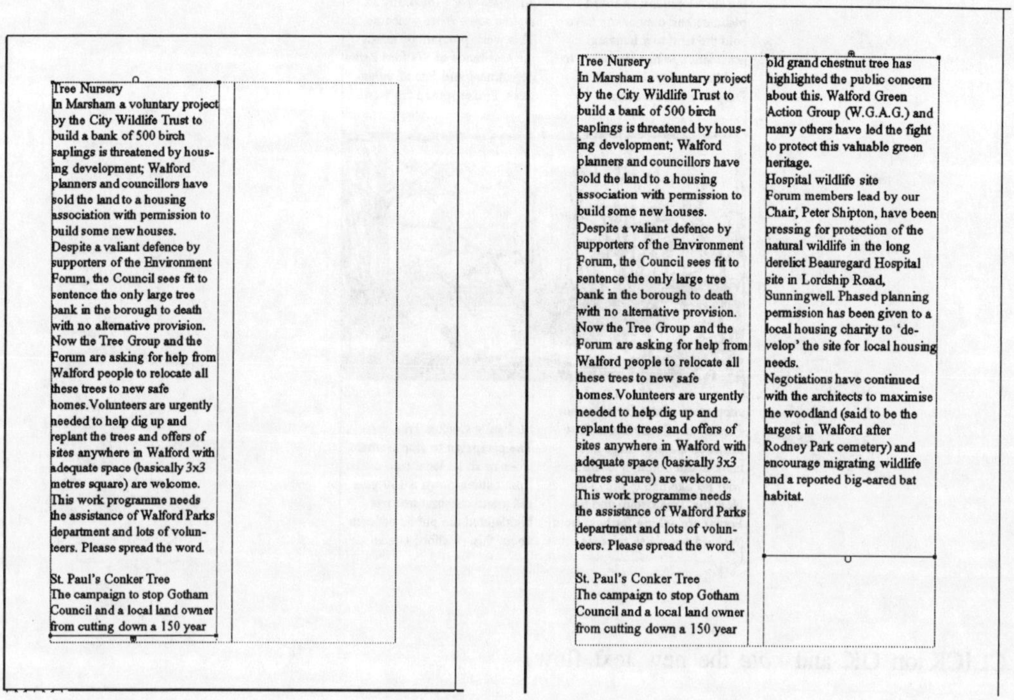

8 With the second column selected, PRESS [Del]. SELECT the first text box and DELETE it.

Activity 25.2 Using Place... for text and pictures with Autoflow on

1 TOGGLE **Options, Autoflow** on.

2 PLACE **GREEN3.TXT** again in the same position and note that it now flows down the second column also.

3 With zero point set to the top left-hand corner of page (default), DRAG out a horizontal guide to **78** mm.

4 PLACE **COMMON2.TIF** so that the top of the graphic is aligned with the guide.

5 With **COMMON2.TIF** selected, PRESS [Shft] and DRAG the handles to rescale the picture and fit it between the page margins and the guide.

6 With the picture still selected, SELECT **Element, Text wrap...** and CLICK on the jump-over icon in the middle of the first row. *Note* the 4 mm default standoff.

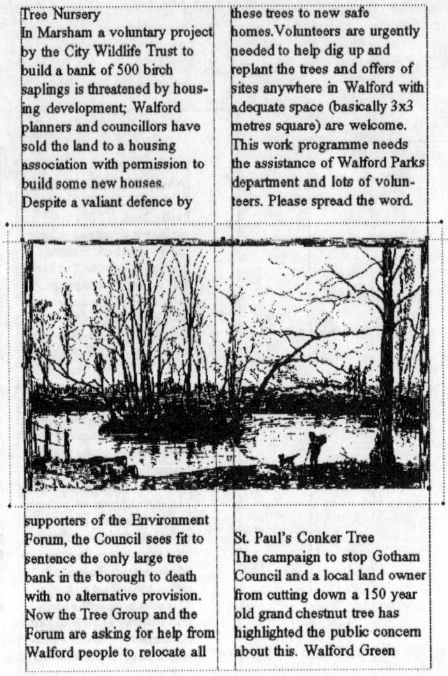

Tree Nursery
In Marsham a voluntary project by the City Wildlife Trust to build a bank of 500 birch saplings is threatened by housing development; Walford planners and councillors have sold the land to a housing association with permission to build some new houses. Despite a valiant defence by supporters of the Environment Forum, the Council sees fit to sentence the only large tree bank in the borough to death with no alternative provision. Now the Tree Group and the Forum are asking for help from Walford people to relocate all these trees to new safe homes. Volunteers are urgently needed to help dig up and replant the trees and offers of sites anywhere in Walford with adequate space (basically 3x3 metres square) are welcome. This work programme needs the assistance of Walford Parks department and lots of volunteers. Please spread the word.

St. Paul's Conker Tree
The campaign to stop Gotham Council and a local land owner from cutting down a 150 year old grand chestnut tree has highlighted the public concern about this. Walford Green

7 CLICK on OK and *note* the new text flow.

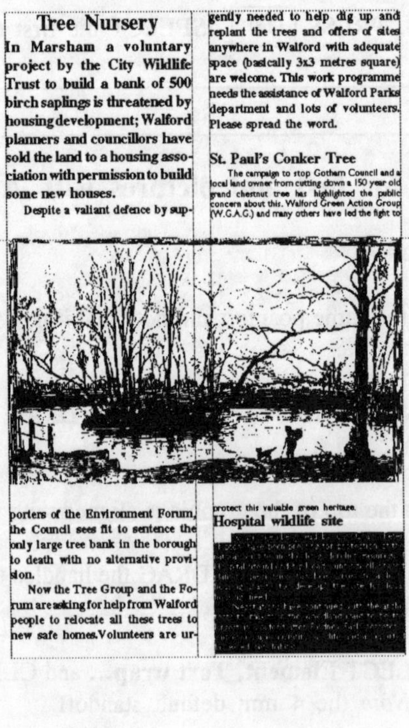

Tree Nursery

In Marsham a voluntary project by the City Wildlife Trust to build a bank of 500 birch saplings is threatened by housing development; Walford planners and councillors have sold the land to a housing association with permission to build some new houses.

Despite a valiant defence by supporters of the Environment Forum, the Council sees fit to sentence the only large tree bank in the borough to death with no alternative provision.

Now the Tree Group and the Forum are asking for help from Walford people to relocate all these trees to new safe homes. Volunteers are urgently needed to help dig up and replant the trees and offers of sites anywhere in Walford with adequate space (basically 3x3 metres square) are welcome. This work programme needs the assistance of Walford Parks department and lots of volunteers. Please spread the word.

St. Paul's Conker Tree

The campaign to stop Gotham Council and a local land owner from cutting down a 150 year old grand chestnut tree has highlighted the public concern about this. Walford Green Action Group (W.G.A.G.) and many others have led the fight to protect this valuable green heritage.

Hospital wildlife site

Activity 25.3 Copying styles from a previous publication and applying them to the current document

1 TOGGLE on **Window, Style palette.**

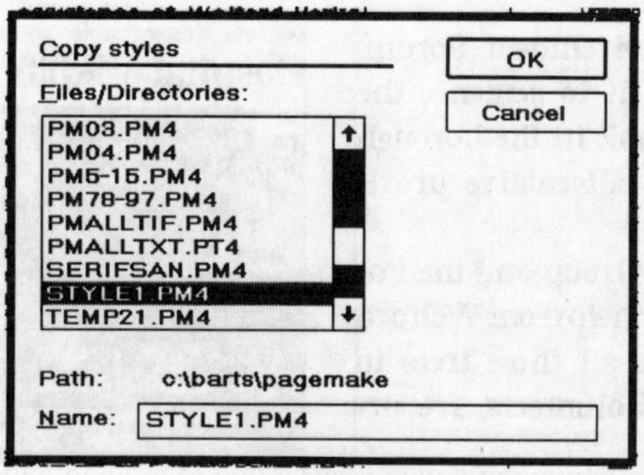

2 SELECT **Type, Define styles** and Copy.

3 SELECT **STYLE1**. CLICK OK. The following alert appears:

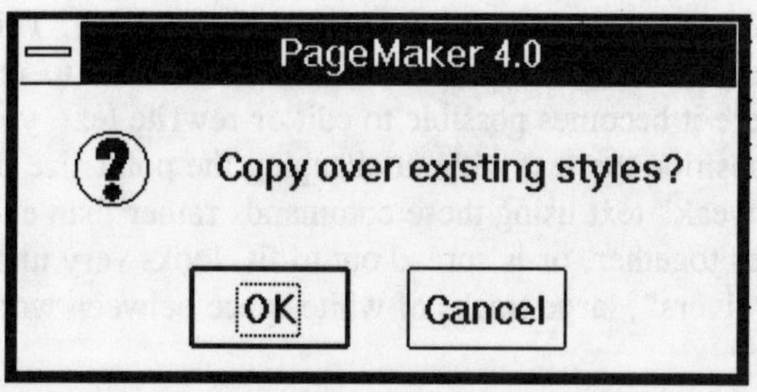

4 CLICK on OK. Style1 **Style palette** is now added to the current document's **Style palette.**

5 SELECT the first line and CLICK on the default style: Subhead1.

6 PRESS Shft + Ctrl + C to centre text and *note* that the style for this paragraph has been modified and is now listed as Subhead1+.

7 SELECT the first paragraph and CLICK on Serif intro in the **Style palette.**

8 APPLY Serif body to the second and third paragraphs. SAVE document as **NEWSLET1.**

9 APPLY Subhead2 to the second and third headings. SELECT the remaining text and APPLY Sans body.

Task 26 Using tracking and leading

➢ **This task shows you how to fit text more precisely by using tracking and leading**

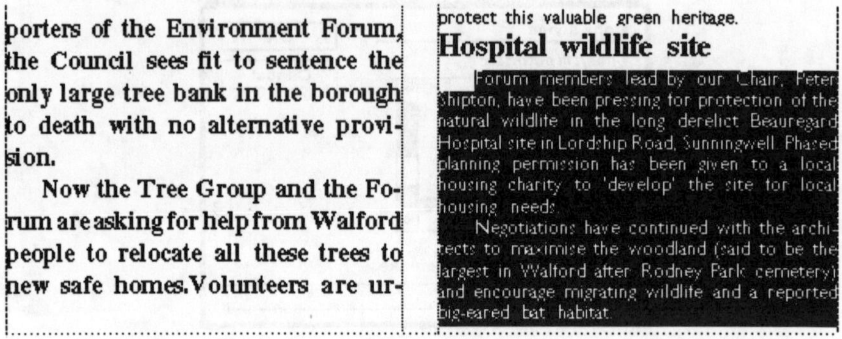

Depending on your target printer, you will notice that odd fragments of text in the last page you have worked on fall at the end of paragraphs and that lines of text in the two columns are not aligned.

This often happens, but needs to be tidied up to make your layout more professional.

Generally it is always best to cut, edit, or rewrite copy to fit. This is not always possible: the better, or tighter, the text, the harder it is to change it easily. In these cases, where it becomes possible to edit or rewrite text, you can use **Leading** and **Tracking** to reposition the text without changing the point size or font. It is often a temptation to "tweak" text using these commands rather than editing it, but text which suddenly bunches together, or is spread out to fit, looks very unprofessional. Beware particularly of "rivers", large tracks of white space between words and lines of justified

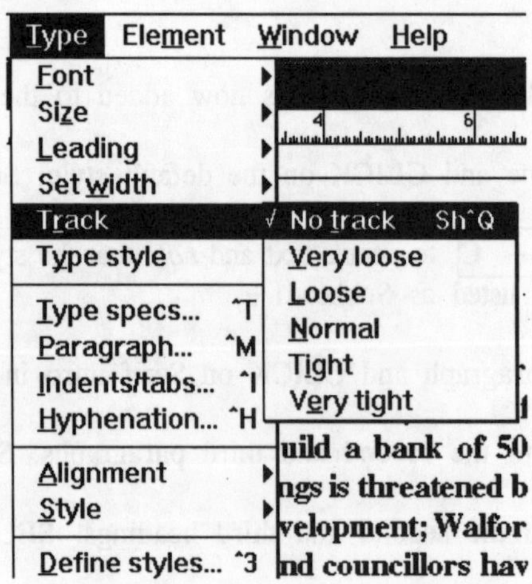

text which distract the reader. You should use tracking to correct these.

Leading is the amount of space between each line of text. The word comes from the slug of lead inserted by typesetters on the old hot-metal machines. The usual default is Auto:, the setting determined by the original type design. If you need to change the leading, apply it to the whole story if at all possible, not to individual lines because it is likely to ruin your type alignment between adjacent columns which look bad. Do not reduce leading below the point size of the text because it may cause one line to over-print the one above.

Tracking is the distance between letters and words. PageMaker gives you the following choices: **No track** uses the original type design specifications; the mis-titled **Normal** makes special adjustments for the proportions of large or small characters but often makes little difference for ordinary sizes such as 10 point. **Very tight** and **Very loose** should be used with care and are probably best reserved for special visual effects in, for example, headlines.

Tracking can be used to remove *orphans* and *widows*. These are printers' terms for, respectively, a line of type on its own at the top or bottom of a page and a single word or word fragment isolated on a single line at the top of a column. Both can be controlled by the use of **Paragraph...** options but tracking often gives you much more control over text flow. If you have time, experiment with both.

Activity 26.1 Applying tracking to align text

1 SELECT the second paragraph of the first story on page 2 of **NEWSLET1**.

2 SELECT **Type, Tracking, Normal** and *note* how the text now flows in four lines, not five.

Activity 26.2 Applying leading to align text

1 SELECT the text of the third story.

2 SELECT **Type, Leading** and SCROLL to select **7.5** points and note how the text is repositioned.

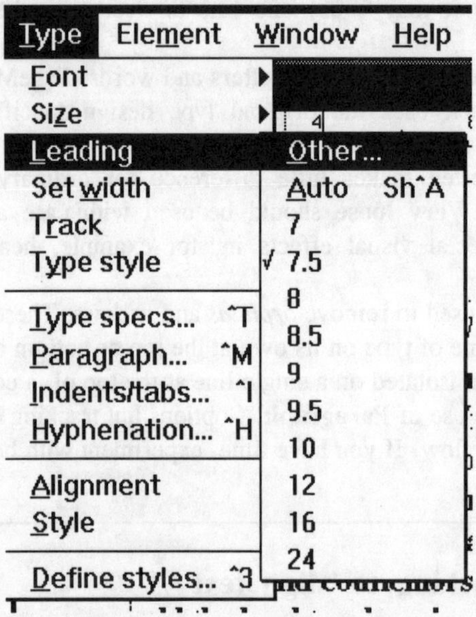

3 SELECT the first sentence of the third story and PRESS Ctrl + Shft + B to set it as Bold.

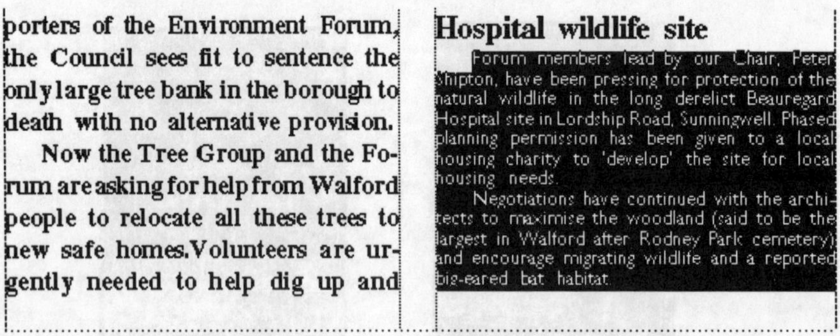

4 PRESS Ctrl + M and TYPE **0** in Indents: First to remove the paragraph indent.

5 Your page should now resemble the example on the following page.

Tree Nursery

In Marsham a voluntary project by the City Wildlife Trust to build a bank of 500 birch saplings is threatened by housing development; Walford planners and councillors have sold the land to a housing association with permission to build some new houses.

Despite a valiant defence by supporters of the Environment Forum, the Council sees fit to sentence the only large tree bank in the borough to death with no alternative provision.

Now the Tree Group and the Forum are asking for help from Walford people to relocate all these trees to new safe homes. Volunteers are urgently needed to help dig up and replant the trees and offers of sites anywhere in Walford with adequate space (basically 3x3 metres square) are welcome. This work programme needs the assistance of Walford Parks department and lots of volunteers. Please spread the word.

St. Paul's Conker Tree

The campaign to stop Gotham Council and a local land owner from cutting down a 150 year old grand chestnut tree has highlighted the public concern about this. Walford Green Action Group (W.G.A.G.) and many others have led the fight to protect this valuable green heritage.

Hospital wildlife site

Forum members lead by our Chair, Peter Shipton, have been pressing for protection of the natural wildlife in the long derelict Beauregard Hospital site in Lordship Road, Sunningwell. Phased planning permission has been given to a local housing charity to 'develop' the site for local housing needs.

Negotiations have continued with the architects to maximise the woodland (said to be the largest in Walford after Rodney Park cemetery) and encourage migrating wildlife and a reported big-eared bat habitat.

Task 27 Creating a runaround

➢This task shows you how to fit text around a cut-out graphic

You have already used Standoff to create a space between graphics and text. PageMaker also gives you the facility to create a runaround where text runs around the outline of a picture or graphic. This can be a very effective way of combining text and pictures.

It is very simple to do, although if the outline is complex, it may be quite time-consuming (PM4 has no facility for doing this automatically). Click anywhere on the standoff line and you will create a handle. Drag that handle and the standoff line will stretch in whatever direction or distance you pull it. The more complex the outline, the more handles you will need to create.

One point you may need to watch is that if you split a column of text in two with a picture or graphic (whether or not it has a runaround) it is very hard to read because the eye has to jump over the picture to scan across a single line. If you have one column, place the picture to the right or left of text. If you are using two or more columns place the picture between two columns.

Activity 27.1 Drawing a runaround

1 With **GN1** open, INSERT a new page 3 and set one column (page 2 will not be affected).

2 If you have been able to save a scan of **COMMON3.TIF**, retrieve it from the sub-directory where you have stored it and PLACE it on the page. SCALE the image to fit within the left, top and bottom margins and CROP the right-hand side to the right margin.

3 SELECT the picture and **Element, Text wrap...** and then the middle icon in the top (*Wrap option:*) row and the right-hand icon in the second (*Text flow:*) row.

4 POINT the mouse about half-way down the right-hand standoff line and CLICK to create a new handle.

5 DRAG the handle diagonally to the left.

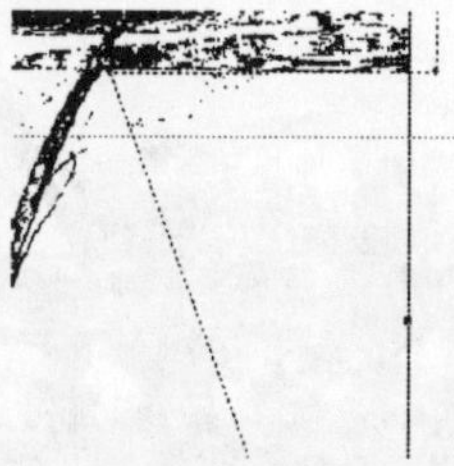

6 CLICK on the standoff line to create as many handles as you need and DRAG the standoff around the curve of the tree in the picture.

7 PLACE **GREEN4.TXT** below and to the right of picture and *note* the way the text flows around the standoff.

8 FORMAT the text heading with Subhead1 style and the remaining text with Serif body.

9 SAVE the document as **GN1** and PRINT. It should resemble the example on the following page.

Plant a new Tree

Please get involved by contacting these addresses and help make Walford a much greener and healthier place to live.

Walford Tree Group: Kate De Selincourt. Tel: 988 8331

Walford Council Arboriculture Officer. Tel: 800 0297

Tree Preservation Order (TPO) forms from: William Douglas. Tel: 8027 8196

Tree Preservation Council, 35 Moscow Square, London SW1 X 8QN: Tel: 235 9954

The Wildflower Trust, 80 Manchester Way, London N1 9AG. Tel: 263 6502

Task 28 Creating bullets

➢ This task shows you how to use a symbol (bullet) to emphasise points in text

Bullets are a common typographical device used to draw attention to points in a list or to indicate that a long story has finished. You can create them simply by using Ctrl + Shft + 8 , or by using Wingdings or Zapf Dingbat fonts, if available.

Bullets are usually round black blobs (hence the name), but with the Wingdings font supplied with Windows you can use any symbol that you like.

Wingdings (or the original Zapf Dingbat font) will not appear in the Story editor, only in the layout view. You can type each one in individually, but this involves calling up **Type**, **Font**, **Wingding** every time and even using the shortcut Ctrl + T it is a tedious process if you have a number to do.

It is much quicker and easier to type in an unusual keyboard character such as # or @ where you want the bullets to occur and then use **Edit, Change...** and the Attributes... Font option to change any occurence of that character into a suitable Wingding symbol.

In this exercise you will also be formatting text and using drag and **Place....** As mentioned above, dragging the screen pointer as you **Place...** a picture will distort the picture to fit the area you have outlined with the screen pointer. It is always wise to use guides to make sure that you have outlined exactly the right area.

Activity 28.1 Using Edit, Change to create bullets

1 With **NEWSLET1** open, INSERT two pages after page 3.

2 TOGGLE on **Autoflow** and PLACE **DIARY.TXT** at the top of page 4 of the document.

3 With the pointer tool selected, TREBLE CLICK to open Story editor.

4 SELECT **Edit, Change** and **Attributes.....**

5 SELECT **Change: Font** and SCROLL to Wingdings. CLICK on OK.

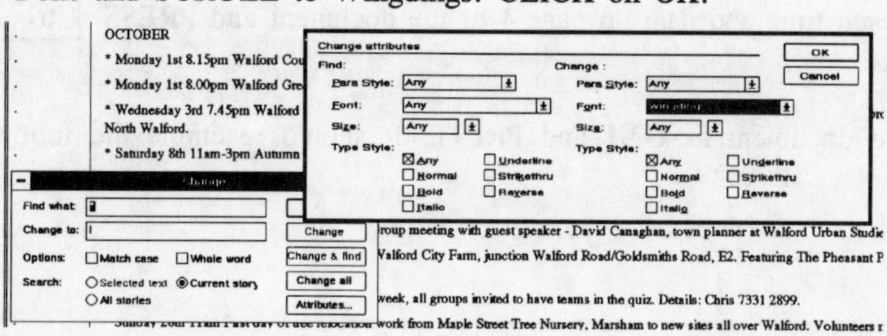

6 TYPE * in the Find what: box. TAB to Change to: and TYPE l. CLICK on OK.

7 CLICK on the PageMaker **Title bar** to return to your layout and observe the changes.

8 REPEAT steps 4 to 7 using Find what: **@** and Change to: **'W'** in the Symbol font.

Activity 28.2 Formatting text and dragging picture

1 APPLY Headline style to "Autumn Diary", "Publications" and "Recycling in Walford".

2 APPLY Subhead1 to "SEPTEMBER", "OCTOBER", "NOVEMBER" and Subhead2 to "Walford Green Guide" and "Paperbox".

3 FORMAT all body text, except the last six lines, with Serif body. FORMAT the last six lines with Sans body.

4 DRAG out horizontal guides to **75** mm and **110** mm below the top margin.

5 PRESS Ctrl + D . POINT the mouse at the intersection of the top guide and the left-hand margin and drag across to the right-hand-guide and down to the lower guide. APPLY a **4** mm standoff to the picture.

6 SELECT the second paragraph under "SEPTEMBER" and SET **Type, Track, Normal.** REPEAT with the sixth paragraph under "OCTOBER".

7 APPLY a **Leading** of **10.5** to all body text except the last six lines on page 5.

8 APPLY (default) tabs to align the last six lines.

9 SELECT each time and date on page 4 of the document and PRESS Ctrl + Shft + U to underline.

10 SAVE the document as **GN1** and PRINT. It should resemble the following examples.

AUTUMN DIARY

SEPTEMBER

● <u>Wednesday 12th, 7pm</u> **Walford Environment Forum: Annual General Meeting and quarterly meeting on current issues and planning.**

● <u>Wednesday 19th 7.30pm</u> **Walford Green Action Group (W.G.A.G.) Public meeting on Energy Conservation and Global Warming at Walford Urban Studies Centre, B, Lower Clayton Road, E5. Buses 253, 10, 38, 22, 48,**

OCTOBER

● <u>Monday 1st 8.15pm</u> **Walford Council Cleaning and Highway Sub-Committee. Walford Town Hall, Hare St. Public access.**

● <u>Monday 1st 8.00pm</u> **Walford Green Action Group (W.G.A.G.) Social at Tandy Hall pub, Sunningwell High St, N1B.**

● <u>Wednesday 3rd 7.45pm</u> **Walford Green Group meeting with report from Annual policy conference and announcement of meeting with prospective parliamentary candidates for North Walford.**

● <u>Saturday 8th 11am-3pm</u> **Autumn Fair at Sunningwell Community Centre, Lester Road. Stalls, refreshments. All welcome.**

● <u>Tuesday 9th 6pm</u> **Walford Council Planning Sub-Committee, Town Hall.**

● <u>Tuesday 18th 6pm</u> **Walford Council Environmental Strategy Sub-Committee, Town Hall, E8.**

● <u>Wednesday 17th 8pm</u> **Walford Green Action Group meeting with guest speaker – David Canaghan, town planner at Walford Urban Studies Centre, Lower Clayton Rd, E5.**

● <u>Saturday 20th 7.30pm</u> **Annual Barn Dance at Walford City Farm, junction Walford Road/Goldsmiths Road, E2. Featuring The Pheasant Pluckers dance band.**

● <u>Sunday 21st</u> **Antarctica Week. Quiz night this week, all groups invited to have teams in the quiz. Details: Chris 7331 2899.**

● <u>Sunday 28th 11am</u> **First day of tree relocation work from Maple Street Tree Nursery, Marsham, to new sites all over Walford. Volunteers needed, equipment provided. Details from Walford Tree Group.** ***See front page.***

NOVEMBER

● <u>Monday 5th 6.15pm</u> **Walford Council Planning Sub-Committee.** <u>7.30pm</u> **Walford Council Environmental Services Committee.**

● <u>Saturday 17th 11am</u> **Walford Book and Record Fair at General Booth Hall, Red Lion Square. Organised by the Walford Green Action Group. Details and offers to Maya on 254 7880.**

● <u>Wednesday 21st 7.45pm</u> **Walford W.G.A.G Strategy meeting, Sunningwell Community Centre, 61 Lester Rd, N16.**

● <u>Saturday 24th-2nd</u> **National Tree Week. General details from: The Tree Preservation Council, Tel: 775 8854. Publicity from W.E.F.**

● <u>Sunday 25th 12-3pm</u> **Christmas Green Fair,** ***venue to be confirmed.***

PUBLICATIONS

Walford Green Guide

The first issue of the Walford Green Guide is planned for next April, in time for Environment Week. All affiliated groups of the Forum will be invited to contribute copy and advertising as well as other services in Walford. Information, artwork, ideas and support are very welcome. Please contact Mary Slattering, 117a Sunnybrook Road, E5. Tel: 809 6101.

Paperboox catalogue

A new glossy twenty page catalogue of recycled paper products is available from suppliers: Paperboox Ltd., Unit 2, Albert Triangle Business Centre, Alice St, E3 4NP. Tel: 985 5230. W.E.N. is printed on recycled paper from Paperboox, so you know it's OK.

Recycling in Walford

A large 140 page spiral bound report produced by Walford Council researcher, Geoffrey Sheridan, which crashed onto table tops in mid-summer. It is an impressive survey of current and future plans if Walford Council has the will to take them up.

Recommendations cover five pages and include:

- Ω Total waste exported from Walford should be steadily reduced and paid by the ton and not according to a preset (high) standard charge.
- Ω More bottle bank sites and new newspaper igloos to be brought into community use.
- Ω Bring in Save-A-Can system for both steel and aluminium cans.
- Ω Involve voluntary groups, schools, charities and business in steady expansion and publicity of new recycling schemes across the borough.

Task 29 Text rotation, Force justify, Paragraph rules and automatic page numbering

➢ **This task demonstrates how to rotate text, stretch text and set page numbers automatically.**

PageMaker allows you to rotate text in four directions. It is very straightforward, if rather limited, but once text is rotated you cannot edit it in layout view, only in the Story editor.

Pictures cannot be rotated in PM4. This has to be done in a paint program and the resulting graphic placed in PM4 as an imported file.

This task also incorporates some other formatting commands: **Force justify** which spreads out characters along a text box, and **Paragraph...** spacing and rules which allows you to include spacing and lines above or below paragraphs automatically.

There is plenty of flexibility in these paragraph options, but be careful of the auto default on rules. If your leading is the same as your point size the rules will run over your last line of text.

Finally, PageMaker has a simple technique for automatic page numbering which you will use here. Open the master pages, position the cursor where you want the page numbers to appear and type Ctrl + Shft + 3 . On a left-hand page this will come up as LM, on a right-hand page RM. You can format this with any font, style or type size that you wish, and automatic page numbering will come up on each document page. (This has already been done on preceding illustrations of pages from **GN1**.)

Use guides to place the LM and RM text boxes so that they are symmetrical; do not place them too close to the text or the edge of the page where they may be trimmed off or get lost in your printer's *grip* (the white space where laser printers hold the paper).

Activity 29.1

Rotating text and using Force justify

1 OPEN page 1 of **GN1** and COPY "Walford Green News". (Ignore the rule and Wingdings).

2 INSERT a page after page 5 and, with the zero point set to the top left-hand corner of the page (default), DRAG down horizontal rulers to **10, 15, 45, 60, 130** and **205** mm and vertical rulers to **20, 24, 65, 119, 125** and **134** mm.

3 PASTE the text below the top guide, CUT the second line and PASTE it so that text sits on the lowest guide on the bottom of the page.

4 COPY the text at the top of the page and PASTE it anywhere on the page. With the pointer tool, SELECT the pasted text and then **Element, Rotate** and CLICK on the second icon.

5 DRAG the rotated text so that the final character ("...D") is aligned with the 60 mm guide and the top edge of the characters is aligned with the left-hand guide.

6 REPEAT steps 3 and 4 with the text on the bottom of the page, ALIGN rotated text with the right-hand guide and the first letter with the 45 mm horizontal guide.

7 SELECT the text box on the bottom of the page and DRAG its handles to align with the width of page margins.

8 HIGHLIGHT the text on the bottom of the page and SELECT **Type, Alignment, Force justify**.

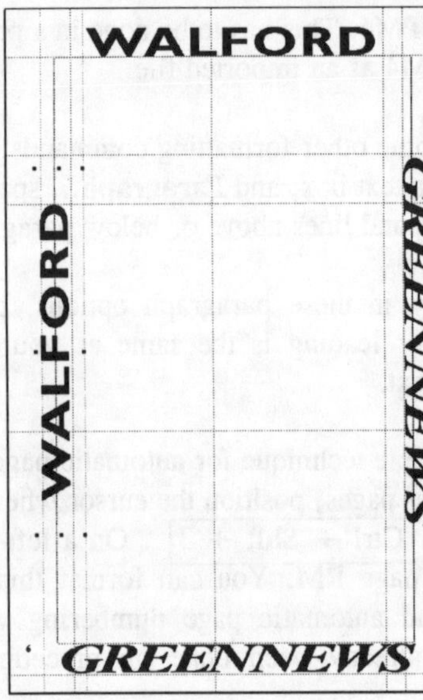

Activity 29.2 Using Place... and Drag with text

1 PLACE **GREEN4.TXT** by dragging the mouse in the area between vertical guides **24** and **119** mm and horizontal guides **10** and **205** mm.

2 PLACE **HELI.TIF** at the intersection of the **65** mm and **130** mm guides, and APPLY text wrap with a 4 mm (default) standoff.

3 FORMAT the top heading ("Clarissa Park...") with Subhead1 style and the other two headings with Subhead2 style.

4 HIGHLIGHT the third heading ("Regular Group...") and then PRESS Ctrl + Shft + C to centre it.

5 APPLY Serif intro style to the first paragraph of body text and Serif body to the second paragraph.

6 SELECT the body text the of the second story and APPLY Sans body style.

7 FORMAT the body text of the third story as **GillSans**, **10** point with **10** point leading.

8 HIGHLIGHT the first three words of the body text of the third story and PRESS Ctrl + Shft + B to set it as Bold.

9 REPEAT step 8 with the first four words of the second paragraph of the third story.

Activity 29.3 Setting rules and space below paragraphs

1 HIGHLIGHT the first paragraph of the third story and PRESS Ctrl + M to open the Paragraph… dialogue box.

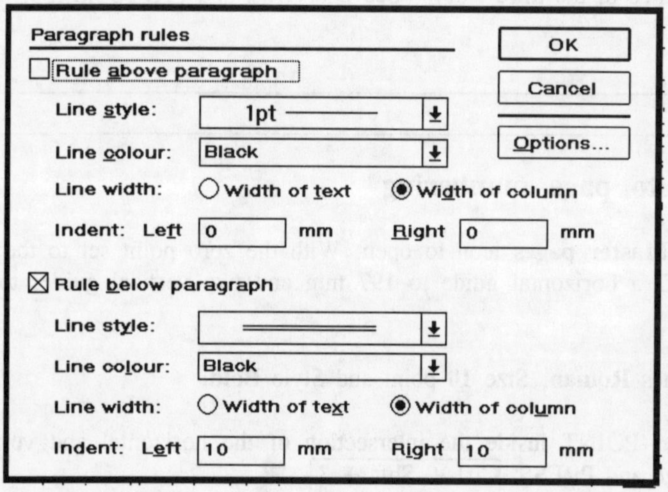

2 CLICK on the Rules, Options… box and CLICK on the Rules below paragraph box. SCROLL to the double rule in the Line style: box and TYPE **10** mm in both the Left indent: and Right indent: boxes.

3 CLICK on the Options box and TYPE **5** mm in Bottom:. CLICK OK to return to the Rules Box, and CLICK OK again to return to the Paragraph… dialogue box.

4 CLICK on the Paragraph space: After option box and TYPE **3** mm. CLICK OK.

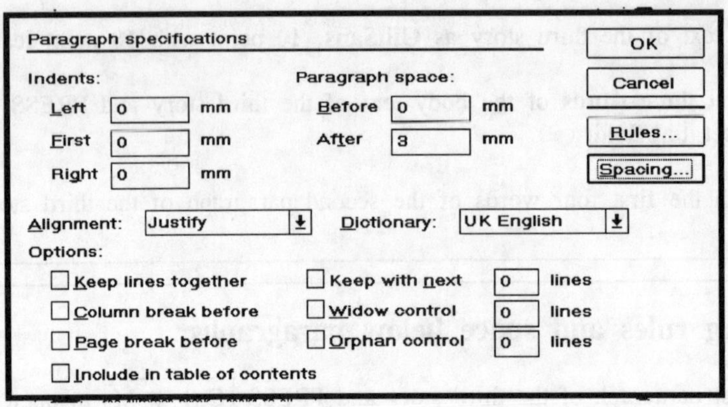

5 HIGHLIGHT the last sentence of the third story ("See Diary...") and PRESS Ctrl + Shft + I to set it as italics.

Activity 29.4 Setting auto page numbering

1 DOUBLE CLICK on the **Master pages** icon to open. With the zero point set to the left-hand corner of the page, DRAG a horizontal guide to **197** mm and two vertical guides to **10** and **285** mm.

2 SELECT Type, Font, **Times Roman**, Size **10** point and Style **Bold**.

3 With the text tool selected POINT inside the intersection of the horizontal and vertical guides on the left-hand page and PRESS Ctrl + Shft + 3.

4 REPEAT on the right-hand **Master page** inside the intersection of the horizontal and

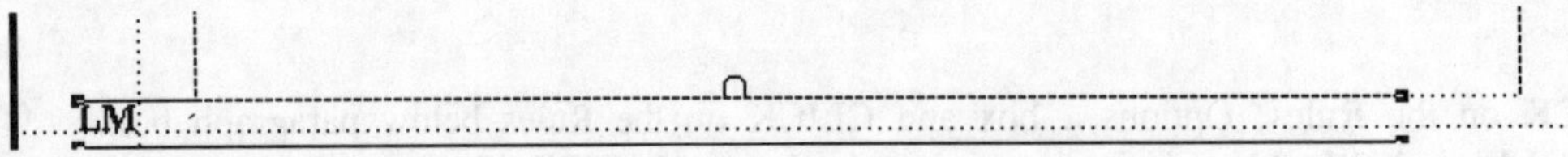

vertical guides.

5 OPEN document pages and note the automatic page numbering.

6 SAVE the document as **GN1** and PRINT. Your work should resemble the example on the following pages.

WALFORD

WALFORD

GREEN NEWS

Clarissa Park Floodlit Pitch kicked out

Another scheme dreamt up by Walford leisure planners to build giant floodlighting and an all-weather football pitch into an historic corner of Clarissa Park has been defeated.

Clarissa Park Users Group, along with Forum support, welcomed local planners' and councillors' rejection of the threat to the beauty of this listed conservation area.

Helipad Threat to Valley fought off

The campaign to stop the Sunningwell Valley Park from gaining planning permission to run three helicopter pads on Walford's eastern border may be over by the time you read this.

Newington Forest planners rejected their application for one next to the Sunningwell Bridge Ice Rink in late August. The application for one next to the Eastway Cycle circuit came before Walford's planning committee on September 10th where rejection was expected. The third application was for one next to the cycle circuit in Marsham. We hope that application receives a similar fate.

Thanks are due to the firm stand taken by Walford Marsh Users Group and M11 campaigner Reg Smithson from the Eastway district who have kept the opposition pressure up over the last few months. W.E.A.G.'s petition kept the pressure up over the summer break. Thanks to all.

Perhaps the Sunningwell Park Authority could get back to dealing with leisure provision from now on.

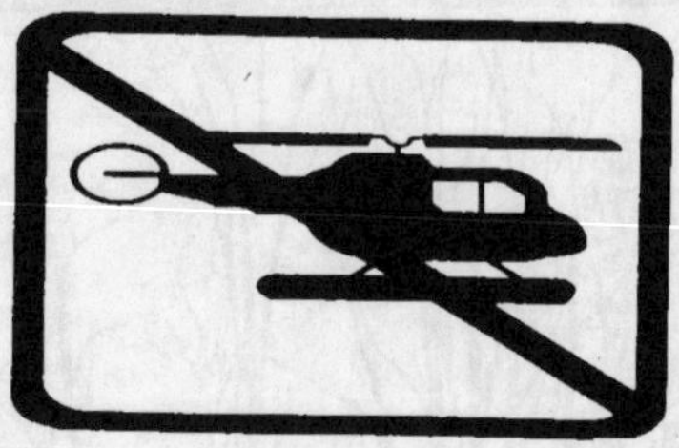

Regular Group meetings

Clean-up Walford Group meets every second Tuesday, monthly at 19, Elring Rd, E8. Monthly clean-ups around Walford every last Sunday. Offers of help, ideas for site clean ups to Mike: 994 9477.

Walford Green Action Group meets bimonthly, first Monday of the month. Next meeting: 3rd November, upstairs at Pembroke Tavern, Walford Downs Junction, 8pm. Contact: Christopher: 733 1298. *See Diary for events.*

GREEN NEWS

Appendix 1

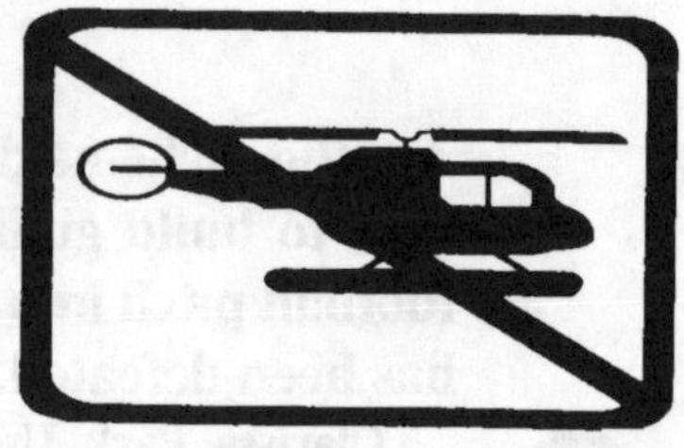

HELL.TIF

LOGO.TIF

ILLUS1.TIF

COMMON2.TIF

COMMON1.TIF

FRIEND.TXT

THIS IS A PRINTING OFFICE
CROSSROADS OF CIVILIZATION
REFUGE OF ALL THE ARTS
AGAINST THE RAVAGES OF TIME
ARMOURY OF FEARLESS TRUTH
AGAINST WHISPERING RUMOUR
INCESSANT TRUMPET OF TRADE
FROM THIS PLACE WORDS MAY FLY
ABROAD
NOT TO PERISH ON WAVES OF SOUND
NOT TO VARY WITH THE WRITER'S HAND
BUT FIXED IN TIME
HAVING BEEN VERIFIED IN PROOF

FRIEND YOU STAND ON SACRED GROUND

COMMON3.TIF

Appendix 2

ADDRESS.TXT

AUTUMN 1993 No. 18 Free to Residents of Walford. Published by Walford Green Action Group 071 - 999 9999

GREEN1.TXT

THE annual Tree Week starts at the end of November when a national focus on tree renewal is organised. We hope to participate in this and urge local people to adopt a local tree, protect existing trees by sending local Tree Preservation Orders to the Planning department and generaly welcoming new tree growth, especially in those areas so badly lacking them - maybe even in your street or on your estate?
The importance of growing more trees cannot be over-emphasised. They provide valuable cover, soak up dirt, dust and noise and trap carbon dioxide gas, not to mention their role in wildlife support.

GREEN2.TXT

AUTUMN is the time for planting trees and clearing up after them. Walford claims to be a Greener borough because of its large open spaces, mainly Gotham Marshes and the Sunningwell Valley, parts of which are under serious threat of commercial development. But there are large areas of the borough sadly lacking in green cover. Many housing estates and streets are bare of trees or large bushes. The summer drought has meant that many trees have become weakened and new trees have died.
The recently-formed Walford Tree Group has done excellent work in campaigning to restore and protect this green shield from the assaults of inner-city conditions.

CONTENTS.TXT

Contents....

GREEN3.TXT

Tree Nursery

In Marsham a voluntary project by the City Wildlife Trust to build a bank of 500 birch saplings is threatened by housing development; Walford planners and councillors have sold the land to a housing association with permission to build some new houses.
Despite a valiant defence by supporters of the Environment Forum, the Council sees fit to sentence the only large tree bank in the borough to death with no alternative provision.
Now the Tree Group and the Forum are asking for help from Walford people to relocate all these trees to new safe homes. Volunteers are urgently needed to help dig up and replant the trees and offers of sites anywhere in Walford with adequate space (basically 3x3 metres square) are welcome. This work programme needs the assistance of Walford Parks department and lots of volunteers. Please spread the word.

St. Paul's Conker Tree

The campaign to stop Gotham Council and a local land owner from cutting down a 150 year old grand chestnut tree has highlighted the public concern about this. Walford Green Action Group (W.G.A.G.) and many others have led the fight to protect this valuable green heritage.

Hospital wildlife site

Forum members lead by our Chair, Peter Shipton, have been pressing for protection of the natural wildlife in the long derelict Beauregard Hospital site in Lordship Road, Sunningwell. Phased planning permission has been given to a local housing charity to 'develop' the site for local housing needs.
Negotiations have continued with the architects to maximise the woodland (said to be the largest in Walford after Rodney Park cemetery) and encourage migrating wildlife and a reported big-eared bat habitat.

GREEN4.TXT

Plant a new Tree

Please get involved by contacting these addresses and help make Walford a much greener and healthier place to live.

Walford Tree Group: Kate De Selincourt Tel: 988 8331

Walford Council Arboriculture Officer

Tel: 800 0297

Tree Preservation Order (TPO) forms from: William Douglas Tel: 8027 8196

Tree Preservation Council, 35 Moscow Square, London SW1 X 8QN Tel: 235 9954

DIARY.TXT

AUTUMN DIARY

SEPTEMBER

* Wednesday 12th, 7pm Walford Environment Forum: Annual General Meeting and quarterly meeting on current issues and planning.
* Wednesday 19th 7.30pm Walford Green Action Group (W.G.A.G.) Public meeting on Energy conservation and Global Warming at Walford Urban Studies Centre, B, Lower Clayton Road E5. Buses 253, 10, 38, 22, 48, etc.

OCTOBER

* Monday 1st 8.15pm Walford Council Cleaning and Highway Sub-Committee. Walford Town Hall, Hare St. Public access.
* Monday 1st 8.00pm Walford Green Action Group (W.G.A.G.) Social at Tandy Hall pub, Sunningwell High St, N1B.
* Wednesday 3rd 7.45pm Walford Green Group meeting with report from Annual policy conference and announcement of meeting with prospective parliamentary candidates for North Walford.
* Saturday 8th 11am-3pm Autumn Fair at Sunningwell Community Centre, Lester Road. Stalls, refreshments. All welcome.
* Tuesday 9th 6pm Walford Council Planning Sub-Committee, Town Hall.
* Tuesday 18th 6pm Walford Council Environmental Strategy Sub-Committee, Town Hall, E8.
* Wednesday 17th 8pm Walford Green Action Group meeting with guest speaker - David Canaghan, town planner at Walford Urban Studies Centre, Lower Clayton Rd, E5.
* Saturday 20th 7.30pm Annual Barn Dance at Walford City Farm, junction Walford Road/Goldsmiths Road, E2. Featuring The Pheasant Pluckers dance band. Tickets: ú5 Children ú2.60 Concessionaries ú3
* Sunday 21st Antarctica Week. Quiz night this week, all groups invited to have teams in the quiz. Details: Chris 7331 2899.
* Sunday 28th 11am First day of tree relocation work from Maple Street Tree Nursery, Marsham to new sites all over Walford. Volunteers needed, equipment provided. Details from Walford Tree Group. See front page.

NOVEMBER

* Monday 5th 6.15pm Walford Council Planning Sub-Committee. 7.30pm Walford Council Environmental Services Committee.
* Saturday l7th 11am. Walford Book and Record Fair at General Booth Hall, Red Lion Square. Organised by the Walford Green Action Group. Details and offers to Maya on 254 7880.
* Wednesday 21st 7.45pm Walford W.G.A.G Strategy meeting, Sunningwell Community Centre, 61 Lester Rd., N16.
* Saturday 24th-2nd National Tree Week. General details from: The Tree Preservation Council, Tel: 775 8854. Publicity from W.E.F.
* Sunday 25th 12-3pm Christmas Green Fair, venue to be confirmed.

PUBLICATIONS

Walford Green Guide
The first issue of the Walford Green Guide is planned for next April, in time for Environment Week. All affiliated groups of the Forum will be invited to contribute copy and advertising as well as other services in Walford. Information, artwork, ideas and support are very welcome. Please contact Mary Slattering, 117a Sunnybrook Road, E5 Tel: 809 6101.
Paperboox catalogue
A now glossy twenty page catalogue of recycled paper products is available from suppliers: Paperboox Ltd., Unit 2, Albert Triangle Business Centre, Alice St, E3 4NP. Tel: 985 5230. W.E.N. is printed on recycled paper from Paperboox, so you know it's OK.
Recycling in Walford

A large 140 page spiral bound report produced by Walford Council researcher, Geoffrey Sheridan, which crashed onto table tops in mid-summer. It is an impressive survey of current and future plans if Walford Council has the will to take them up.

Recommendations cover five pages and include:

@ Total waste exported from Walford should be steadily reduced and paid by the ton and not according to a preset (high) standard charge.

@ More bottle bank sites and new newspaper igloos to be brought into community use.

@ Bring in Save-A-Can system for both steel and aluminium cans.

@ Involve voluntary groups, schools, charities and business in steady expansion and publicity of new recycling schemes across the borough.

GREEN5.TXT
Clarissa Park Floodlit Pitch
kicked out

Another scheme dreamt up by Walford leisure planners to build giant floodlighting and an all-weather football pitch into an historic corner of Clarissa Park has been defeated.
Clarissa Park Users Group, along with Forum support, welcomed local planners' and councillors' rejection of the threat to the beauty of this listed conservation area.

Helipad Threat to Valley fought off
The campaign to stop the Sunningwell Valley Park from gaining planning permission to run three helicopter pads on Walford's eastern border may be over by the time you read this.
Newington Forest planners rejected their application for one next to the Sunningwell Bridge Ice Rink in late August. The application for one next to the Eastway Cycle circuit came before Walford's planning committee on September 10th where rejection was expected. The third application was for one next to the cycle circuit in Marsham. We hope that application receives a similar fate.
Thanks are due to the firm stand taken by Walford Marsh Users Group and M11 campaigner Reg Smithson from the Eastway district who have kept the opposition pressure up over the last few months. W.E.A.G.'s petition kept the pressure up over the summer break. Thanks to all.
Perhaps the Sunningwell Park Authority could get back to dealing with leisure provision from now on.

Regular Group meetings
Clean-up Walford Group meets every second Tuesday, monthly at 19, Elring Rd, E8. Monthly Clean-ups around Walford every last Sunday, offers of help, ideas for site clean ups to Mike: 994 9477.
Walford Green Action Group meets bimonthly, first Monday of the month. Next meeting: 3rd November upstairs at Pembroke Tavern, Walford Downs Junction 8pm. Contact: Christopher: 733 1298. See Diary for events.

Index

PageMaker shortcuts

Action	Menu/Command	Shortcut (Ctrl +keystroke)	Page
Copy selected text or item	**Edit, Copy**	**^C**	39
Cut and copy selected item**	**Edit, Cut**	**^X**	39
Help	**Help, Index**	***F1***	xiii
Import text or picture file	**File, Place...**	**^D**	41
New document	**File, New...**	**^N**	2
Open document	**File, Open...**	**^O**	8
Page numbering, automatic	**Master pages**	**^ + Shft + 3**	99
Page size on screen:	**Page, Fit in window**	**^W**	4
	Page, Actual size	**^1**	3
Paragraph format	**Type, Paragraphs**	**^M**	67
Paragraph indents	**Type, Indents/tabs**	**^I**	77
Paragraph style palette	**Window, Style palette**	**^Y**	80
Paste copy of text or item	**Edit, Paste**	**^V**	23,39
Print	**File, Print**	**^P**	20
Quit and close program	**File, Exit**	**^Q**	6
Rulers	**Options, Rulers**	**^R**	47
Save document	**File, Save**	**^S**	6
Select all text/items on page	**Edit, Select all**	**^A**	15
Story editor	**Edit, Edit Story**	**^E**	55
Tabs	**Type, Indents/tabs**	**^I**	77
Type specifications (all)	**Type, Specs...**	**^T**	57
Undo last action	**Edit, Undo**	**^Z**	37
View all pasteboard		**^ + Shft + W**	83